SCRIPTURE

and the

AUTHORITY

of

GOD

SCRIPTURE
and the
AUTHORITY
of
GOD

How to Read the Bible Today

N. T. WRIGHT

This is a revised and expanded version of a book
previously published as *The Last Word*.

HarperOne
An Imprint of HarperCollinsPublishers

HarperOne

Library of Congress Cataloging-in-Publication Data

Wright, N.T. (Nicholas Thomas)
    Scripture and the authority of God: how to read the Bible today / N.T.Wright —
    1st ed.
    p. cm.
    ISBN 978-0-06-201195-4
    1. Bible–Evidences, authority, etc.   1. Title.
BS480.W83 2005
220.1'3—dc22   2005040380

11   12   13   14   15   RRD(H)   10   9   8   7   6   5   4   3   2   1

For Stephen Sykes and Robin Eames

CONTENTS

PREFACE TO THE AMERICAN EDITION

Writing a book about the Bible is like building a sandcastle in front of the Matterhorn. The best you can hope to do is to catch the eye of those who are looking down instead of up, or those who are so familiar with the skyline that they have stopped noticing its peculiar beauty.

But clearly we have to do something to grab people's attention and make them take a fresh look at some old questions. People used to talk about "the battle for the Bible," and in the last generation we have seen the Bible used and abused, debated, dumped, vilified, vindicated, torn up by scholars, stuck back together again by other scholars, preached from, preached against, placed on a pedestal, trampled underfoot, and generally treated the way professional tennis players treat the ball. The more you want to win a point, the harder you hit the poor thing.

Taken as a whole, the church clearly can't live without the Bible, but it doesn't seem to have much idea of how to live with it. Almost all Christian churches say something in their formularies about how important the Bible is. Almost all of them have devised ways, some subtle, some less so, of ostentatiously highlighting some parts of the Bible and quietly setting aside other parts. Does this matter? If not, why not? If so, what should we do about it?

In response to those questions, let me return to the Matterhorn and the sandcastle. I have taken part in many discussions over the years about what the Bible is and what place it should occupy in Christian mission and thinking. As I have done so, I have increasingly come to the conclusion that there are many people outside and inside the church who need to be nudged to look up once more with fresh eyes, not just at the foothills, but at the crags and crevasses, at the cliffs and snowfields, and ultimately at the dazzling and dangerous summit itself. What that all means in terms of the Bible will, I hope, become clear as we proceed.

In particular, the question of how the Bible can be "authoritative" has echoed through a thousand recent debates in the life of the worldwide church. We have only to mention the question of sexual ethics to see at once how important, and yet how difficult, the question of biblical authority can be. We have only to think of the so-called Jesus wars in North America to see how much controversy can still be generated by the question of whether the four gospels in the New Testament are in any sense reliable as presentations of who Jesus was and why he died. And we need only mention Dan Brown's runaway bestseller *The Da Vinci Code* to remind ourselves that questions about how Christianity began, and whether the New Testament can be trusted on that point, are clearly issues on which our whole culture can still be thrown into turmoil.

And that's only the New Testament. What about the Old—the "Hebrew scriptures," as they are sometimes called? Here we still find huge misunderstandings. Some Christians seem to regard the whole Bible, from Genesis to Revelation, as equally authoritative and valid—even though Jesus himself, according to the gospels themselves, seems to have set aside the food laws and posed severe questions about the observance of the sabbath; even though Paul is shrill in his insistence that the ancient command to circumcise male children is no longer relevant for followers of Jesus; and even though the Letter to the Hebrews makes it abundantly clear that the detailed regulations about the Temple and the sacrificial system have been made redundant by the single sacrifice of Christ, the

great High Priest. Other Christians, meanwhile, have taken Paul's
saying that "Christ is the end of the Law" as giving them cheerful
permission to ignore anything and everything in the Old Testament. Is there a way through this problem?

Having made the Bible the focus of my own professional work
for many years, I have become convinced that we are asking at
least some of the questions in the wrong way. In an earlier article,
I explored one of the central questions: How can what is mostly a
narrative text be authoritative? (This article, "How Can the Bible
Be Authoritative?" was published in *Vox Evangelica* 21, 1991, 7–32,
and, like some other things I have written over the years, is now
available at www.ntwrightpage.com.) I then developed my argument in terms of seeing the biblical story as a five-act play, with
ourselves called to improvise the concluding act, in chapter 5 of
The New Testament and the People of God (Fortress Press, 1992). This
present little book builds on those two earlier attempts and tries to
set out the question in a new way.

I have tried, in particular, to face head-on the question of how
we can speak of the Bible being in some sense authoritative when
the Bible itself declares that all authority belongs to the one true
God and that this is now embodied in Jesus himself. The risen
Jesus, at the end of Matthew's gospel, does not say, "All authority
in heaven and on earth is given to the books you are all going to
write," but "All authority in heaven and on earth is given to me."
This ought to tell us, precisely if we are taking the Bible itself as
seriously as we should, that we need to think carefully what it
might mean to think that the authority of Jesus is somehow exercised through the Bible. What would that look like in practice? In
particular, what happens when we factor in Jesus's own redefinition
of what "authority" itself might mean?

For this new edition I have added two chapters to try to make it clear, with a couple of case studies, how this redefinition might work out. The two topics I have chosen—the sabbath and monogamy—have not been particularly hot topics in recent discussion, and for that reason they may be better places to think through the wider issues than some of the subjects over which passions are easily aroused. I am under no illusions that I have said the last word on these subjects, but I suspect that for many Christians, they will at least open up trains of thought that should be useful both in themselves and in illustration of the larger theme. I am grateful to the publishers for this chance to expand the range of the book.

I have been particularly spurred to write this book by participating in two commissions which have been looking at the nature of "communion" (as in the phrase "the Anglican Communion") and to which, naturally, questions about the Bible have been central. The International Anglican Doctrinal and Theological Commission met under the chairmanship of Bishop Stephen Sykes from 2001 to 2008. The Lambeth Commission, chaired by Archbishop Robin Eames, met three times in 2004 and published its findings (the Windsor Report) on October 18 of that year. The central thrust of the present book was developed, in conversation with my colleagues, as part of the work of both these groups, and the overlap of some passages here with some paragraphs of the Windsor Report is an indication of my indebtedness to my colleagues and the conversations which forced me to think through issues afresh and to clarify what I was trying to say. I dedicate this book to Stephen and Robin with profound gratitude for the way in which they have handled the lively discussions on both commissions, and for thereby helping me to think more deeply into the relevant issues.

The present book makes no pretense at completeness, in terms either of the topics covered or of the debate with other writers that might be expected. It is more a tract for the times. I trust that those who have grumbled at the length of some of my other books will not now grumble at all the things I have left unsaid in what is necessarily a very compressed, at times almost telegraphic, treatment. I would like to think that I might one day return to the topic at more leisure, not least in order to interact with the many writers from whom I have learned a great deal and who may spot that their ideas are being borrowed, or perhaps engaged with, in the pages that follow. In addition, I am extremely grateful to those who read the text and commented on it at short notice: Dr. Andrew Goddard, Professor Richard Hays, Dr. Brian Walsh, and my brother Dr. Stephen Wright. They are not responsible for what I say, and indeed will continue to disagree with me at certain points, but they have helped me greatly in making things clear. I am grateful as always to SPCK, and specifically to Simon Kingston, Joanna Moriarty, Sally Green, Yolande Clarke, and Trisha Dale for their help at various stages of the work.

I have written of the "Old Testament" and the "New Testament," fully aware that many today regard those phrases as inadequate or prejudicial, preferring phrases like "Hebrew scriptures" (though some are in Aramaic) and "Christian scriptures." I write as a Christian, and from the beginning, as I shall argue, followers of Jesus Christ regarded the ancient Israelite scriptures as having reached a climactic fulfillment in Jesus himself, generating the "new covenant" prophesied by Jeremiah. We cannot pretend to a neutral set of labels. I hope that this, and other linguistic details, will not distract anyone from what I am actually saying.

The prologue sets the scene, putting the discussion about the Bible into its context within church history and then into the context of contemporary culture. Those who already know all this, or who are eager to get to the heart of what I want to say, could if they wish, skip to chapter 1, where the story really starts.

My own church has for centuries used a wonderful prayer which I make my own in completing this task:

Blessed Lord, who hast caused all holy Scriptures to be written for our learning, grant that we may in such wise hear them, read, mark, learn, and inwardly digest them, that by patience and comfort of thy holy Word we may embrace and ever hold fast the blessed hope of everlasting life which thou hast given us in thy Son, our Savior Jesus Christ. Amen.

Tom Wright
Auckland Castle

PROLOGUE

The place and role of the Bible within the church's mission and common life is once again being heavily contested. Current "battles for the Bible" in various parts of the church—not least, but not only, within debates about sexual ethics—need to be understood as part of much wider issues in the church and the world. Until we recognize this fact, understand it and deal with it, we will go on finding that discussions about the authority of scripture, let alone about particular passages and topics, will remain a dialogue of the deaf.

But before I tackle these issues directly, I must cover some preliminary matters—hence, a prologue.

First, then, a brief sketch of the place of the Bible within the Christian church, to be followed by a look at the role of scripture within contemporary culture.

Scripture within the Church

THE FIRST 1,500 YEARS

The Bible has always been central to the life of the Christian church. Jesus himself was profoundly shaped by the scriptures he knew, the ancient Hebrew and Aramaic texts whose stories, songs, prophecy and wisdom permeated the Jewish world of his day. The earliest Christians searched those same scriptures in their effort to understand what the living God had accomplished through Jesus, and in their eagerness to reorder their life appropriately. By the early second century many of the early Christian writings were being collected, and were themselves treated with reverence and given a similar status to the original Israelite scriptures. By the end of the second century some of the greatest Christian minds were making the study and exposition of scripture, both the ancient Israelite texts and the more recent Greek ones written by Jesus's followers, a major part of their work in pursuing the mission of the church and strengthening it against persecution without and controversy within. Though we often think of subsequent writers like Origen, Chrysostom, Jerome and Augustine—and, much later, Aquinas, Luther and Calvin—as great "theologians," they would almost certainly have seen themselves first and foremost as Bible teachers. Indeed, the modern distinction between "theology" and "biblical studies" would never have occurred to any of them.

THE REFORMATION TO THE PRESENT

The sixteenth-century Reformers appealed to scripture over against the traditions which had grown up in the church during the Middle Ages; the churches which stem from the Reformation all emphasize (as the early fathers had done) the central importance of the Bible. Whether Lutheran or Reformed, whether Anglican, Presbyterian, Baptist or Methodist, or whether the newer Pentecostal churches, all officially accord scripture the central place in their faith, life, and theology. This has marked out the post-Reformation churches from the Eastern Orthodox and Roman Catholic churches, which give a more complex and interwoven account of how scripture operates within the life of the church. But those older churches, too, have never shrunk from the insistence that scripture remains the written word of God. Indeed, they have been known to criticize the post-Reformation churches not only because of differences in the interpretation of specific texts, but also because of what seems to them a cavalier attitude to scripture itself.

DEVOTION AND DISCIPLESHIP

Scripture has never, in any major part of the Christian church, been simply a book to be referred to when certain questions are to be discussed. From the very beginning it has been given a key place in the church's worshipping life, indicating that it has been understood not only as part of the church's *thinking* but also as part of the church's *praise and prayer*. As well as the obvious use of the Psalms at the heart of Christian worship in many traditions, the reading of the gospel within the eucharistic liturgy in many if not most branches of the church indicates the implicit but powerful belief that the Bible continues to be both a central way in which God addresses his people and a central way in which his people respond. The widespread habit of private reading and study of scripture, once a more particularly Protestant phenomenon but now widely encouraged among Roman Catholics as well, has a long track record as a central part of Christian devotion.

Not only devotion: discipleship. Reading and studying scripture has been seen as central to how we are to grow in the love of God; how we come to understand God and his truth more fully; and how we can develop the moral muscle to live in accordance with the gospel of Jesus even when everything seems to be pulling the other way. Since these remain vital aspects of Christian living, the Bible has been woven into the fabric of normal Christian life at every point.

Different churches have developed different ways of making this theory a reality. My own church (the Church of England, part of the Anglican Communion) has classically expressed its beliefs about scripture not by writing massive treatises or doctrinal compendia on every possible issue, as though to close things down and relieve ordinary Christians of the need to read, think, and pray with a fresh mind. Rather, it has insisted that reading scripture remains the focal point of its public worship. It has encouraged all Christians to read and study scripture for themselves. And it has charged its leaders, particularly its bishops, with the central and solemn task of studying and teaching scripture and ordering the life of the church accordingly.

Scripture within Contemporary Culture

The Bible doesn't live just within the church, because the church (if it is true to its own nature and vocation) is always open to God's world. Our contemporary culture impinges on the questions that are being asked about the Bible, and does so in a variety of ways.

I want next to look at five areas of contemporary culture, each of which interacts with the others in complex interlocking patterns: culture, politics, philosophy, theology, and ethics. This list is by no means exhaustive, but it gives an indication of why it is intrinsically difficult, not least in the Western world today, to use scripture in a way which will command recognition and assent across the church, let alone before the watching world.

SCRIPTURE AND CULTURE

The continuing and much-discussed interplay between "modern" and "postmodern" *culture* has created a mood of uncertainty within Western society at least. There are three areas that can be easily identified.

First, the big, older *stories* of who we are and what we're here for have been challenged and deconstructed. This is, in a sense, turning modernism's rhetoric on itself. Modernism (the movement which began with the eighteenth-century Enlightenment) made its way, through writers like Voltaire, by attacking the big, overarching story told by the church. Postmodernity has now done the same to all the great stories by which human beings order their lives ("metanarratives"), not least the stories of "progress" and "enlightenment" which modernism itself made its stock-in-trade. The Bible, rather obviously, not only offers some fairly substantial individual stories about God, the world and humankind, but in its canonical form, from Genesis to Revelation, tells a single overarching story which appears to be precisely the kind of thing people today have learned to resist. Like all metanarratives, it is instantly suspected of being told in order to advance someone's interest. It is, people suspect, some kind of a power play.

Second, the notion of *truth* has been under scrutiny and indeed attack. Many today operate with two quite different types of "truth." If we asked, "Is it true that Jesus died on a cross?" we normally would mean, "Did it really happen?" But if we asked, "Is the parable of the Prodigal Son true?" we would quickly dismiss the idea that "it really happened"; that is simply not the sort of thing parables are. We would insist that, in quite another sense, the parable is indeed "true" in that we discover within the narrative a picture of God and his love, and of multiple layers of human folly, which rings true at all kinds of levels of human knowledge and experience.

So far, so good—though most people do not always stop to muse over these different senses of "true" and their implications for other questions. Instead, late modernity has tried to squeeze more and more areas of human discourse into the first type of "truth," making a "fact" out of everything and thereby trying to put everything into the kind of box which can be weighed, measured, and verified as if it were an experiment in the hard sciences like chemistry, or even an equation in mathematics. But this attempt has overreached itself, not least in areas like history and sociology. Now postmodernity has pushed us in the other direction: toward supposing that all "truth," including the supposed "facts" of scientific experiment, can be reduced to power-claims (the scientists were, perhaps, working for a firm which wanted to make money by selling a particular kind of drug, and so forth). All claims to truth thus collapse into claims to power, as Nietzsche argued over a century ago. All statements about "the way things are" turn into variations on "the way I see them," or even "the way it suits me to see them."

Or perhaps we should insist on saying "the way we (in a particular culture) see them." The idea of "social construction," in which what look at first sight like settled, quantifiable concepts are shown up to be "just the way this particular society constructs its view of reality," has deeply affected the way we understand "truth" as a whole. Since the Bible has quite a lot to say about truth—and since it also has plenty to say about how particular individuals relate to that truth—it has become easy to imagine that its claims can and should be reduced to particular, and highly relative and situational, angles of vision. "What's true for you" may not be the same as "what's true for me"; the "social construction of reality" may be very different from one society to another. This cultural move, which would have been incomprehensible to many people until quite recently, now appears so obvious to people in our world that, paradoxically, it has itself become one of the absolute and unquestionable truths of our day.

Third, we have faced the problem of *personal identity*. The question "Who am 'I'?" can no longer be answered as easily as once it could. No longer "the master of my fate, the captain of my soul," the individual looks within and discovers a seething ebb and flow of different impulses. Heisenberg's uncertainty principle, which boils down in popular discourse to saying that the very act of observing things changes the things you observe, works just as well, worryingly, when you look in the mirror. The Bible has a good deal to say about who we are as human beings, and/or as members of God's people, and/or as followers of Jesus—not least that we are made in God's image and called to be people in whom that image is being renewed. We thus find that to hold in our minds and hearts what the Bible says about who we are, and to do our best to live by that, clashes head-on with our culture, which questions and challenges not only the Christian view of who we are, but all fixed and settled views of personal identity.

Thus (a) understanding the world, (b) understanding reality, and (c) understanding myself all threaten to collapse into a morass, a smog of unknowing, of not even knowing what "knowing" itself might mean. For people who experience the world and themselves like that—and a glance at most newspapers or magazines will show that this is the cultural air many people breathe all the time—uncertainty about everything is a way of life. This uncertainty in turn, of course, begets a new and anxious eagerness for certainty: hence the appeal of fundamentalism, which in today's world is not so much a return to a premodern worldview but precisely to one form of modernism (reading the Bible within the grid of a quasi- or pseudoscientific quest for "objective truth"). Every single aspect of this impinges on the reading of scripture in general and its use in church in particular. In this book I shall be arguing neither for a variety of modernism, nor for a return to premodernism, nor yet for a capitulation to postmodernism, but for what I hope is a way through this entire mess and muddle and forward into a way of living in and for God's world, and within the community of God's people, with Christian and biblical integrity.

SCRIPTURE AND POLITICS

Culture impinges, obviously, on the second area: *politics*. Reality has harsh ways of reaffirming itself: someone draws a line in the sand in the Middle East, or in a road in Northern Ireland, and someone else gets shot if they cross it.

The horrible tragedy of September 11, 2001, was on the one hand a classic postmodern moment (the great symbols of modernist economic and military empire being literally deconstructed by an embodied alternative story). That tragedy was on the other hand also a reassertion of solid reality, not least of death itself, over against a world which thought it could go on reinventing itself and generating infinite varieties of private space for its own amusement and profit.

Political questions press upon us. Contemporary Western democracy is in crisis: more people vote in "reality TV" shows than in some major elections; genuine debate is sterilized by over-large majorities, by the Cabinet's stifling of parliamentary debate, by spin doctors, and by undemocratic lobbying. The left/right spectrum (which many assume to be part of the fixed order of reality, but which was in fact inherited merely from the French Revolution) compels parties, commentators, and voters into an inappropriate "package deal" mentality where it is assumed that once you decide on one issue you are committed to a particular position on lots of others as well. The older models for discovering who we all were and what we all ought to be doing (e.g., that of the Cold War) have disappeared, leaving it painfully obvious that we had no idea what would happen next and thus had no game plan to cope with it (hence the Balkans, the Middle East and especially Israel/Palestine, famine, AIDS, and other disasters).

The map of what we might call political morality has shrunk.

The Holocaust and the nuclear bomb have cast a moral shadow over the last fifty years; virtually all Western moral and political debate has taken place in a world where we know certain things are wrong but aren't sure how to put them right. The main impulse has been to be as unlike Adolf Hitler as possible—a noble aim, no doubt, but not terribly helpful in coming to grips with details in a very different world. Not all the issues we face can be understood in terms of a rerun of the 1930s. Powerful and important movements such as feminism and postcolonialism, often gaining energy from the postmodern impulse, but often also creating their own new and "certain" moralities ("political correctness"), tug at our sleeves at every corner.

What happens when we read the Bible within this world? We find that its narratives of exodus and conquest, of liberation and monarchy, of exile and return, and of the universal claims of Jesus—of, in fact, the Kingdom of God!—set off multiple new resonances which we cannot and must not ignore. But two centuries of pretending that the Bible has nothing to say about politics (i.e., since the Enlightenment, when this became axiomatic) have left the church disabled—in a way which theologians from Irenaeus in the second century to Richard Hooker in the sixteenth simply would not recognize—when it comes to serious, responsible contemporary rereadings that will address the urgent political issues of our day.

SCRIPTURE AND PHILOSOPHY

Culture and politics send us back, third, to *philosophy*. Whether people recognize it or not, the questions philosophy raises lie underneath the great puzzles of each society. How do we know things? Who are we? What sort of account can we give of the world as a whole? Is it a single unity, or must it be divided into some kind of "material" and "spiritual" duality—in which case, which of those two is the more important, the "real" part? What is the nature of evil, and what, if anything, can and should be done about it? How can humans live appropriately within the world? These are some of the classic problems addressed by Western philosophy.

The last two were given a particular answer within the Enlightenment. Among many strands which came together in that cultural explosion was a new way of looking at the problem of evil, which had been highlighted particularly by the wars of religion in the seventeenth century and by the Lisbon earthquake of 1755. Suppose, ran the proposal, that the world is indeed divided into two, with God upstairs and a world of pure causation downstairs. If that is so, God isn't in charge of the daily running of the material world, and he doesn't intervene into it. If he were, and did, then Lisbon (today we might add "and Auschwitz") would seem incomprehensible. But if we leave God out of the equation, and propose that he will instead provide spiritual solace in the present and a spiritual hope for the future, detached from the material world, then the world belongs to, and is in the hands of . . . the human race. More particularly, it belongs to that part which, at exactly the same time as philosophers were thinking these thoughts, was developing new technologies which began to deliver unimagined control over, and opportunities to exploit, the natural world. God's in his heaven; we will solve the world's problems, with our industry, our energy, and (of course) our empires.

Well, we haven't. The Enlightenment failed to deliver the goods. People not only didn't stop fighting one another, but the lands of the Enlightenment became themselves embroiled in internecine conflict, while "rational" solutions to perceived problems included such Enlightenment triumphs as the Gulag and the Holocaust. The greatest of the Enlightenment-based nations, the United States of America, has been left running a de facto world empire which gets richer by the minute as much of the world remains poor and gets poorer. All this, and much besides, goes to make up the fertile soil within which postmodernity has germinated and grown, as a protest movement but also as a kind of philosophy in its own right. The consequent retreat, in twentieth-century philosophy, from the big questions into analytic philosophy on the one hand ("Let's at least be sure we're talking sense, even if we don't know what we're talking about"), and into existentialism on the other ("How can I live authentically within this strange, alien world?"), have likewise proved dead-end streets. What's the point of talking sense in a world of virtual reality where image is everything and substance nothing? What's the point of trying to be "authentic" when I don't know who "I" am from moment to moment?

My present point is that these older ways of thinking about the world have left their mark on the study of the Bible, on the way it has been taught in universities, colleges, and churches, and on many of the books still regarded as standard—and that these ways of thinking have themselves become discredited in mainstream culture. (Plenty of professors still teach the "objective" results of research that has been undertaken "without presuppositions," and regard any attempt to question this as a kind of return to a naive or fundamentalistic precritical mentality.) Now we have a new wave of Bible study, or rather several new waves, in which postmodern movements such as those just mentioned—feminism and postcolonialism, for instance—have provided new angles of vision. As I said, all this is going on, and influencing the way people read the Bible and talk about it, whether or not they are aware of it, perhaps especially if they are not. Is there a way of reading the Bible which is sensitive to the swirling currents of philosophical debate while not allowing itself to be snatched by Scylla or dragged down into Charybdis?

SCRIPTURE AND THEOLOGY

Theology itself, fourth, and the related story of recent biblical study not least in the self-consciously pluralist culture of America, has provided an equally confusing, if now quite rich, context for reading the Bible. The place of the Bible within theology was a frequent subject of debate when the liberal theology of the 1960s and 1970s was at its height, without any answers being given which would today be regarded as firm. Though John A. T. Robinson was hailed as a fine biblical scholar, his most famous book, *Honest to God* (SCM, 1963), showed no sense of obligation to wrestle with the Bible in the course of refashioning ways of thinking Christianly, and indeed saw scripture as part of the problem rather than as part of the solution. The revival of trinitarian theology that has occurred since the 1970s (one thinks of theologians as diverse as Jürgen Moltmann, Colin Gunton, and Rowan Williams) has happened without much detailed explicit engagement with or exegesis of the Bible, perhaps because the biblical scholars available to the systematic theologians were not much interested in the doctrine of God, or indeed in "doctrine" at all for its own sake.

Few if any of the systematic or philosophical theologians of the last couple of generations have written serious works on scripture itself; that is, on what the text actually says. A remarkable and instructive example is the recent book *Holy Scripture: A Dogmatic Sketch,* by John Webster (CUP, 2003); one would never have known, from reading this book, anything at all about what the Bible contains. Webster might respond that this comment misses the point; but since his thesis is that scripture is the central source for all Christian thinking, it might have been appropriate (and not beyond the wit of such a fine scholar) to base this contention, too, on scripture itself. Perhaps theologians have been warned off by the example of Karl Barth, who provided a great deal of exegesis within his *Church Dogmatics,* not much of which has stood up to sustained examination. (Two noble exceptions to this point are A. C. Thiselton, whose massive commentary on 1 Corinthians [Eerdmans, 2000] stands impressively, and in this respect uniquely, beside his two previous tomes on philosophical hermeneutics—*The Two Horizons* [Paternoster, 1980] and *New Horizons in Hermeneutics* [HarperCollins, 1992]; and Oliver O'Donovan, much of whose work, not least his book *The Desire of the Nations* [CUP, 1996] includes sustained reflection on the content, not merely the fact, of scripture.)

Systematic theologians, in fact, have often written about early Christian beliefs as though biblical scholarship were simply a matter of crunching a few Greek roots into shape—or, alternatively, as though the only biblical scholars who mattered were those who managed to "discover" within the biblical text the very ideas which the theologians themselves were looking for. Nobody really believes any more the old idea that biblical scholars, equipped with neutral and objective tools and methods, provide the "facts" about scripture which the systematic theologians can then "interpret." Anyone who has worked within biblical scholarship knows, or ought to know, that we biblical scholars come to the text with just as many interpretative strategies and expectations as anyone else, and that integrity consists not of having no presuppositions but of being aware of what one's presuppositions are and of the obligation to listen to and interact with those who have different ones. But people still sometimes write, when it suits them, as if this old picture were in some sense still true.

Looking wider, the movement which styles itself "radical orthodoxy" has attempted to put forward a kind of restated medieval theology, but the Bible is strangely absent from its scheme. Much of the theology which has come from Africa and other parts of the non-Western world, by contrast, has been richly informed by the Bible, but because until very recently few in the West took it seriously it has failed to make much impact. Within the increasingly important work on the relation of Christianity to Judaism, Islam, Hinduism, and other communities, the Bible has often appeared as something of an embarrassment.

In a fair amount of contemporary theology, in fact, the Bible has often been simply a resource—important, rich, and stimulating in some cases, problematic, and puzzling in others—but without any overall sense of how Christian theology might either live under its authority or offer a theoretical account of what such authority might be. Within biblical study itself, the "Jesus wars" of the 1990s in America, the increasingly contested "new perspective on Paul," and the feminist (and other) highlighting of "texts of terror" (passages in the Bible which have been used to justify violence and oppression) all bear the marks of interaction, often unrecognized, with the cultural, political, and philosophical pressures already noted. With all this going on, one might be forgiven for throwing up one's hands and wondering whether we can get anything out of the Bible except some stimulus for our private devotions. Even then, some critics have suggested that there may be passages that ought to carry a health warning. Is there a way forward?

SCRIPTURE AND ETHICS

Fifth, the questions of *ethics*—the point at which a good deal of debate about scripture and its authority has been focused—are bound up with, or perhaps we should say bouncing off the walls of, all of the above. An obvious example is the somewhat frantic current attempt to reengage with arguments about war and peace.

People who had never heard the phrase "just war" have suddenly discovered the need to think about it—and about biblical impulses, perhaps even gospel imperatives, toward pacifism. Would Jesus have been a pacifist? If he didn't believe in violence, why did he overturn the moneychangers' tables? Does Paul's affirmation of "the powers that be" as ordained by God, and their right to "bear the sword" (Romans 13:1–7), mean that Christians are permitted to serve in the armed forces—something comparatively few Western Christians would have questioned until quite recently?

Likewise, today's questions to do with gender and sexuality have emerged from, and been shaped and reshaped within, the cultural, political, philosophical, and theological contexts of our time. A good example, relevant for our current questions, is the fierce debate between "essentialists" and "constructivists" on the question of homosexuality. The former have insisted on a more or less modernist position about the objective "identity" of the individual, as consisting in his or her sexual "orientation" or preference, and in pursuit of this have continued a relentless quest for a "gay gene." The latter advocate a thoroughly postmodern, free-floating account of sexuality in which the choice of types of activity is made as one goes along, without any need to explain, excuse, or vindicate one's behavior in terms of any external norms, objective reality, or assumption of "identity." This debate plays through in a different key some, though not all, of the old discussions, as between "nature" and "nurture." But how might all this relate, if at all, to the Bible?

A Fresh Word from God

When faced with these five sets of questions, the Christian reading of the Bible ought not simply to be squashed into one shape or another according to local pressure. On the contrary. Jesus's parables broke into the world of first-century Judaism, cracking open ways of understanding God's Kingdom and creating hermeneutical space for fresh insight in which people could imagine different ways of thinking, praying, and living. In the same way, scripture itself holds out the continuing promise that God's word will remain living, active, powerful, and fruitful (e.g., Isaiah 40:8; 55:11; Hebrews 4:12). This should generate the hope that, through a fresh reading and teaching of scripture, our present culture and all that goes with it will be addressed and challenged by new and God-given viewpoints, not simply allowed to neuter them by squashing them into that culture's own mold.

Thus it will not do, within serious debate, simply to appeal (say) to Romans 13 to justify military action, or to Romans 1 to forbid homosexual practice, as though a simple reference settled the question. To do so would be to fail to pay attention both to the real debates that have gone on about the context and meaning of both passages, and to the key underlying questions:

1. In what sense is the Bible authoritative in the first place?
2. How can the Bible be appropriately understood and interpreted?
3. How can its authority, assuming such appropriate interpretation, be brought to bear on the church itself, let alone on the world?

These are the questions to which the rest of this little book is devoted.

These battles over the Bible sometimes echo, and sometimes do not, the sixteenth-century debates about the authority of scripture in relation to "tradition" and "reason." This is confusing, because many Christians in mainline denominations, not least many clergy, learned the theology they know in terms of those debates, and feel under strong pressure to take up positions accordingly. This then becomes a matter of party loyalty. Those of a Protestant or evangelical viewpoint will emphasize the authority of scripture; those from a Catholic context will make a strong case for tradition; those who think of themselves as liberals will emphasize reason.

But "scripture," "tradition," and "reason" themselves, and the relations between them, have not remained static over the centuries. Even scripture, whose text has remained relatively constant (though subject to minor revisions through manuscript discoveries), is now *perceived* very differently from how it was seen in the sixteenth century. Then it was seen as a repository of true doctrine and ethics, and indeed the supreme "authority" for early human and Israelite history in the same sense that Herodotus and Thucydides are the primary "authorities" for early Greek history; now it is variously seen as the miscellaneous collection of documents reflecting one strand of religious and cultural history or, from quite another point of view, as the great narrative, the overarching story of God and the world (see pages 121–127). Similarly, the meaning of the word "tradition," after works such as John Henry Newman's treatment of the development of doctrine, is significantly different from what was meant earlier (pages 71–76). Again, the word "reason," which for Hooker and his contemporaries meant primarily thinking clearly and logically, has gained a capital R and an independent, autonomous identity, and is now often appealed to both as a separate source and as referring to the supposed results of modern science (pages 78–81 and 120–121).

All this means that it would be misleading in the extreme to envisage our present discussions as basically a way of fighting sixteenth-century battles over again. That is not to say that those older divisions do not matter, or that they have nothing in common with today's questions. The extent to which today's divisions are linked with those of the past will emerge in what follows. It is to say that we must delve deeply into the question of what it means in the twenty-first century to be a loyal Christian, and within that a wise and mature reader and/or teacher of scripture, taking full account of the new pressures and challenges we now face. We must draw on wisdom from the past without imagining that our questions are identical with those faced by Luther or Calvin, by Cranmer or Hooker, or for that matter by Aquinas or Ignatius Loyola. Or for that matter, by John Henry Newman, Karl Barth, William Temple, Michael Ramsey, or John A. T. Robinson. We are in uncharted waters. And they are a lot deeper than some contemporary debaters seem to realize.

The Shallow Level of Current Debate

It is sad to report that a good deal of debate is conducted today at a shallow and trivializing level—which ought to be remarkable, considering how much work has been done on the relevant questions. We are all used to, and tired of, the heated exchanges which consist simply of name-calling ("fundamentalist," "radical," and so on). We have all been mired in the tactic of "guilt by association," the attempt to draw up lists of who is on which side by noticing various resemblances in different people's positions even though the issues may be very different. Simplistic affirmations ("The Bible says") on the one hand, and counter-affirmations ("You read the text naively; we read it *in context,* and that changes everything") on the other, only get in the way of serious debate. (See further, chapter 7.)

Similar problems occur when people push the Bible to one side

because it appears to be telling them something they do not wish
to hear. This happens secretly in the case of the so-called conservative, who may well choose to ignore the ecclesial, ecumenical, sacramental, and ecological dimensions of Paul's soteriology, in order
to highlight and privilege a doctrine of justification or "personal
salvation" which owes its real shape to a blend of Reformation,
Enlightenment, romantic, and existentialist influences. It may well
happen in a bold, in-your-face manner in the case of the so-called
radical, who will often take pleasure in saying things like, "Paul says
this, and we now know he's wrong," playing to a gallery stacked
with iconoclasts. All this has to be named, shamed, and gotten rid
of if we are to seek and find fresh wisdom.

Recent Literature

This is not to say that there has not been some thorough, indeed
magisterial, work on the nature of biblical authority. Since I
cannot here interact with it in any detail, or even summarize
different viewpoints, I merely note that I have found help—
albeit sometimes by being forced to disagree!—in a wide variety
of books. Rather than clutter up the text at this point, I have
listed them in the Appendix. They indicate that there is today a
lively and serious engagement with the whole question of what
scripture is, how to read it with cultural and intellectual alert-
ness and integrity, and how to enable it to be what it ought to
be in the life and mission of the church. These works in their
different ways refuse both the sterile either/or of classic modernist polemic and the agonized deconstructions offered by
postmodernity. They represent fresh ways out the other side of
all that, into creative and intelligent reflection. What follows
stands in implicit and, I hope, complementary dialogue with this

emerging movement. I hope that those who want to take the debate forward from where I leave it will not simply shoot from the hip on behalf of one or another well-established point of view, but will be prepared to do business with the serious debate at its cutting edges.

1.

By Whose Authority?

In the prologue we looked first at the role of scripture in the historical Christian church and then at how today's understanding of that role is impacted by contemporary culture. In this first chapter we will look at the "authority of scripture" as part of a larger divine authority.

"Authority of Scripture" Is a Shorthand for "God's Authority Exercised *through* Scripture"

We now arrive at the central claim of this book: that the phrase "authority of scripture" can make Christian sense only if it is a shorthand for "the authority of the triune God, exercised somehow *through* scripture." Once we think this through, several other things become clear.

All authority is from God, declares Paul in relation to governments (Romans 13:1); Jesus says something very similar in John 19:11. In Matthew 28:18, the risen Jesus makes the still more striking claim that all authority in heaven and on earth has been given to him, a statement echoed elsewhere—for instance, in

Philippians 2:9–11. A quick glance through many other texts in both the Old Testament (e.g., Isaiah 40—55) and the New (e.g., Revelation 4 and 5) would confirm this kind of picture. When John declares that "in the beginning was the word," he does not reach a climax with "and the word was written down" but "and the word became flesh." The letter to the Hebrews speaks glowingly of God speaking through scripture in time past, but insists that now, at last, God has spoken through his own son (1:1–2). Since these are themselves "scriptural" statements, that means that scripture itself points—authoritatively, if it does indeed possess authority!—away from itself and to the fact that final and true authority belongs to God himself, now delegated to Jesus Christ. It is Jesus, according to John 8:39–40, who speaks the truth which he has heard from God.

The familiar phrase "the authority of scripture" thus turns out to be more complicated than it might at first sight appear. This hidden complication may perhaps be the reason why some current debates remain so sterile.

This kind of problem, though, is endemic in many disciplines, and we ought to be grown-up enough to cope with it. Slogans and clichés are often shorthand ways of making more complex statements. In Christian theology, such phrases regularly act as "portable stories"—that is, ways of packing up longer narratives about God, Jesus, the church and the world, folding them away into convenient suitcases, and then carrying them about with us. (A good example is the phrase "the atonement." This phrase is rare in the Bible itself; instead, we find things like "The Messiah died for our sins according to the scriptures"; "God so loved the world that he gave his only son," and so on. But if we are to discuss the atonement, it is easier to do so with a single phrase, assumed to "contain" all these sentences, than by repeating one or more of them each time.) Shorthands, in other words, are useful in the same way that suitcases are. They enable us to pick up lots of complicated things and carry them around all together. But we should never forget that the point of doing so, like the point of carrying belongings in a suitcase, is that what has been packed away can then be unpacked and put to use in the new location. Too much debate about scriptural authority has had the form of people hitting one another with locked suitcases. It is time to unpack our shorthand doctrines, to lay them out and inspect them. Long years in a suitcase may have made some of the contents go moldy. They will benefit from fresh air, and perhaps a hot iron.

When we take the phrase "the authority of scripture" out of its suitcase, then, we recognize that it can have Christian meaning only if we are referring to scripture's authority *in a delegated or mediated sense* from that which God himself possesses and that which Jesus possesses as the risen Lord and Son of God, the Immanuel. It must mean, if it means anything Christian, "the authority of God *exercised through* scripture." The question then becomes: What might we mean by the authority of God, or of Jesus? What role does scripture have *within that?* Where does the Spirit come into the picture? And, not least, how does this "authority" actually *work?* How does it relate, if at all, to the "authority" of leaders or office-bearers within the church?

Authority and Story

Before we begin to answer these questions, we must face another complication. Not only does the Bible itself declare that all authority belongs to the God revealed in Jesus and the Spirit; the Bible itself, as a whole and in most of its parts, is not the sort of thing that many people envisage today when they hear the word "authority."

It is not, for a start, a list of rules, though it contains many commandments of various sorts and in various contexts. Nor is it a compendium of true doctrines, though of course many parts of the Bible declare great truths about God, Jesus, the world, and ourselves in no uncertain terms. Most of its constituent parts, and all of it when put together (whether in the Jewish canonical form or the Christian one), can best be described as *story*. This is a complicated and much-discussed theme, but there is nothing to be gained by ignoring it.

The question is, How can a story be authoritative? If the commanding officer walks into the barrack-room and begins "Once upon a time," the soldiers are likely to be puzzled. If the secretary of the cycling club pins up a notice which, instead of listing times for outings, offers a short story, the members will not know when to turn up. At first sight, what we think of as "authority" and what we know as "story" do not readily fit together.

But a moment's thought suggests that, at deeper levels, there is more to it than that. For a start, the commanding officer might well need to brief the soldiers about what has been going on over the past few weeks, so that they will understand the sensitivities and internal dynamics of the peace-keeping task they are now to undertake. The narrative will bring them up to date; now it will be their task to act out the next chapter in the ongoing saga. Or supposing the secretary of the club, having attempted unsuccessfully to make the members more conscious of safety procedures, decides to try a different tack, and puts up a notice consisting simply of a tragic story, without further comment, of a cyclist who ignored the rules and came to grief. In both cases we would understand that some kind of "authority" was being exercised, and probably all the more effectively than through a simple list of commands.

There are other ways, too, in which stories can wield the power to change the way people think and behave—in other words, can exercise power and/or authority. (The relationship between those two concepts is of course another well-known nest of puzzles, but I hope the point I am making is clear enough.) A familiar story told with a new twist in the tail jolts people into thinking differently about themselves and the world. A story told with pathos, humor, or drama opens the imagination and invites readers and hearers to imagine themselves in similar situations, offering new insights about God and human beings which enable them then to order their own lives more wisely.

All of these examples, and many more besides which one might easily think of, are ways in which the Bible does in fact work, does in fact exercise authority. This strongly suggests that for the Bible to have the effect it seems to be designed to have it will be necessary for the church to hear it as it is, not to chop it up in an effort to make it into something else. To this we shall return.

"Authority of Scripture" as the Language of Protest

One more introductory remark on the way in which the phrase "authority of scripture" has functioned and developed in recent centuries. It is my impression that it has emerged in situations of protest, whether that of Martin Luther against the pope, of the great free church movements against Anglicanism (I think of the nineteenth-century Baptist Charles H. Spurgeon appealing to scripture to explain why he opposed so much in the established church), or, within various denominations, of a would-be "biblical" minority against a supposed "liberal" leadership. In other words, the phrase is invoked when something is proposed or done in the church to which others object: "You can't do that, because the Bible says . . ." Of course, there is a positive use as well, exemplified in the teaching and preaching of scripture. But it has often been observed that when people who insist on the authority of scripture have things all to themselves—perhaps by leaving a supposedly unbiblical denomination and setting up on their own—they quickly subdivide into those who read the Bible *this* way against those who read it *that* way. This itself suggests that an over-hasty appeal to scripture all by itself does not in fact work. We need to set scripture within the larger context which the biblical writers themselves insist upon: that of the authority of God himself.

But what does the Bible itself have to say about the authority of God?

Authority in God's "Kingdom"

When we say or hear the word "authority," we by no means always think of the sort of thing that the Bible has in mind when speaking of the way in which the one true God exercises "authority" over the world. Scripture's own preferred way of referring to such matters, and indeed to the saving rule of Jesus himself, is within the more dynamic concept of God's sovereignty, or *Kingdom*. It is not, that is, the kind of "authority" which consists solely in a final court of appeal, or a commanding officer giving orders for the day, or a list of rules pinned up on the wall of the cycling club. This emerges clearly in the gospels, where Jesus's "authority" consists both in healing power and in a different kind of teaching, all of which the gospel writers—and Jesus himself—understood as part of the breaking-in of God's Kingdom. And the notion of God's Kingdom is itself to be understood not, first and foremost, within the very different usage of the last two or three centuries in *our* culture, but within the setting and aspirations of Israel both in the Old Testament (the Psalms, Isaiah, Daniel, and so on) and in the world of Jesus's own day. (I and others have explored this world and these meanings at length: see, e.g., *Jesus and the Victory of God* [Fortress Press, 1996], Part II.)

The biblical writers live with the tension of believing both that in one sense God has always been sovereign over the world and that in another sense this sovereignty, this saving rule, is something which must break afresh into the world of corruption, decay, and death, and the human rebellion, idolatry, and sin which are so closely linked with it. "In that day," says the prophet, "YHWH will be king over all the world; he will be one and his name one" (Zechariah 14:9)—with the clear sense, however paradoxical when speaking of the creator God, that this state of affairs has not yet come about. The Jewish hope was that God's Kingdom would break into their world, to set them free from oppression and put the whole world to rights. When Revelation speaks of God and the Lamb receiving all power, glory, honor, and so forth, it is because through the Lamb's victory the whole of creation is being brought back into its intended harmony, rescued from evil and death. God's *authority*, if we are to locate it at this point, is his sovereign power accomplishing this renewal of all creation. Specific authority over human beings, notably the church, must be seen as part of that larger whole.

This is where I go beyond the very helpful thesis of Telford Work, who examines, in *Living and Active: Scripture in the Economy of Salvation* (Eerdmans, 2002), the way in which scripture functions dynamically within the complex events of human salvation. This is fine as far as it goes. But in scripture itself God's purpose is not just to save human beings, but to renew the whole world. This is the unfinished story in which readers of scripture are invited to become actors in their own right. "The authority of scripture" is thus a sub-branch of several other theological topics: the mission of the church, the work of the Spirit, the ultimate future hope and the way it is anticipated in the present, and of course the nature of the church. Failure to pay attention to all of these in discussing how scripture functions is part of the problem, as we can see when people, hearing the word "scripture," instantly think of a rule-book—and then, according to taste, either assume that all the rules are to be followed without question or assume that they can all now be broken.

The question addressed in Work's book, however, remains the right one: What *role* does scripture play *within* God's accomplishment of this goal? It is enormously important that we see the role of scripture not simply as being to provide *true information about,* or even an accurate running commentary upon, the work of God in salvation and new creation, but as taking an active part *within* that ongoing purpose. If we are to discover a fully rounded—and itself biblical!—meaning of "the authority of scripture," it will be within this setting. Short-circuiting the question of biblical authority by ignoring these opening moves is one of the root causes of our continuing puzzles and polarizations. Scripture is there to be a means of God's action in and through us—which will include, but go far beyond, the mere conveying of information.

Transcending "Revelation"

All this alerts us to the fact that scripture is more than simply "revelation" in the sense of "conveying information"; more even than "divine self-communication"; more, certainly, than simply a "record of revelation." Those categories come to us today primarily from an older framework of thought, in which the key question was conceived to be about a mostly absent God choosing to send the world certain messages about himself and his purposes.

That usurped the richer biblical picture of a present, albeit transcendent, God, celebrating with the rich dynamic life of his creation and grieving over its shame and pain.

Of course, there is a much older notion of "revelation," according to which God is continually revealing himself to and within the world he has made, and particularly to and within his people Israel. This would accord much better with the richer image I have in mind. But in much post-Enlightenment thought this gave way to a shrunken version of the idea, namely a picture of God merely conveying true religious, theological, or ethical information. That, in turn, gave birth to the alternative hypothesis, popular not least within existentialist movements, that scripture was simply the "record" of a revelation which had taken place elsewhere, presumably in events in the life of God's people, or in their personal religious experience. This then gave rise to the false antithesis of seeing scripture either as a convenient repository of timeless truth, a vehicle for imparting "true information," or as a take-it-or-leave-it resource, itself at one remove from the reality of which it spoke, some of which might come in handy from time to time within a strategy whose outline, purpose, and energy derived from elsewhere, but which could be dispensed with, at least in part, if it seemed unhelpful for those purposes. A fully Christian view of the Bible includes the idea of God's self-revelation but, by setting it in a larger context, transforms it. Precisely because the God who reveals himself is the world's lover and judge, rather than its absentee landlord, that self-revelation is always to be understood within the category of God's mission to the world, God's saving sovereignty let loose through Jesus and the Spirit and aimed at the healing and renewal of all creation.

More Than a Devotional Manual

If the Bible is not simply "revelation," neither is it simply a devotional aid, even the primary devotional aid. It does of course play that role within many traditions, including my own. Indeed, I cannot conceive of daily communion with God without scripture at its center. There have been many different traditions of using scripture as the fuel and raw material of personal prayer, adoration, meditation, and so on. The monastic *lectio divina,* the evangelical "quiet time," and the increasingly popular "Ignatian" meditation all provide examples. In those communities that use a daily office, there is often a time of silence following one or all of the readings, designed to allow for prayerful reflection. Such uses of scripture, I fully believe, embody something which is vital for healthy Christian living.

But all this is not primarily what is meant by "the authority of scripture." Confusion can arise at this point, not least within the Protestant emphasis, articulated afresh in some circles today, that "God speaks only through scripture." This arises, I think, in relation particularly to questions of personal guidance, where a warning is being given not to believe or follow ideas and impulses which do not come from, or at least cannot be backed up by, scripture itself.

But it is wrong to confuse *devotion* with *authority.* All sorts of things happen in prayer, not least when it is based on scripture. Connections are made as sparks jump to and fro between a passage of scripture and one's own life and circumstances. Sometimes these are deeply compelling. But by itself this process is neither a sufficient nor a necessary part of letting scripture be *authoritative* in the church. The flying sparks of prayerful interpretation can still, alas, lead us astray. Self-deceit remains a powerful and dangerous possibility (as Wittgenstein said, "Nothing is so difficult as not deceiving oneself"). Those individuals and churches which have "heard God speaking" through a passage of scripture, and have acted accordingly, tend to be those where division is most apparent. Equally, the strong testimony both of scripture itself and of Christian (and other) experience is that God speaks in many and various ways, including through creation itself (Psalm 19; Romans 1:20; 10:18), and supremely through the Living Word, the word become flesh (John 1:14; Hebrews 1:1–2).

God does indeed speak through scripture. But we cannot either reduce God's speech to scripture alone, or for that matter ignore the fact (which much recent writing has emphasized) that "speech" must itself be thought of in terms of "speech-*acts*," the deeds which are performed by the fact of speaking at all, in particular saying certain types of things ("I promise," "I find the defendant innocent," and so on). And we must not confuse the idea of God speaking, in this or any other way, with the notion of *authority*. Authority, particularly when we locate it within the notion of God's Kingdom, is much more than that. It is the sovereign rule of God sweeping through creation to judge and to heal. It is the powerful love of God in Jesus Christ, putting sin to death and launching new creation. It is the fresh, bracing and energizing wind of the Spirit.

In particular, the role of the Bible within the church and the individual Christian life indicates three things which are of central importance as we proceed. To begin with, it reminds us that the God Christians worship is characterized not least as a God who *speaks,* who communicates with his human creatures in words. This differentiates the God of the Old and New Testaments from some other gods known in the worlds of the time, and indeed today. It means that the idea of reading a book to hear and know God is not far-fetched, but cognate with the nature of God himself.

Second, it is central to early Christian instruction that we be transformed by the renewal of our minds (Romans 12:1–2). In other words, it is important that God's transforming grace is given to us not least through enabling us to *think* in new ways. Again, this means that the idea of reading a book in order to have one's life reordered by the wisdom of God is not counter-intuitive, but is cognate with the nature of Christian holiness itself.

Third, it reminds us that the God we worship is the God whose world-conquering power, seen in action in the resurrection of Jesus, is on offer to all those who ask for it in order thereby to work for the gospel in the world (Ephesians 1:15–23). The idea of reading a book in order to be energized for the task of mission is not a distraction, but flows directly from the fact that we humans are made in God's image, and that, as we hear his word and obey his call, we are able to live out our calling to reflect the creator into his world.

2.

Israel and God's Kingdom-People

To put the previous chapter's discussion in context, we must now stand back and reflect on what we mean by God's Kingdom, and then consider the role of scripture within it.

Affirming God's Victory over Evil

The question of God's "Kingdom" or "Kingship" is raised, in the Old Testament and in subsequent Judaism, by the presence of radical evil within the good creation and within the covenant people themselves. How can God be King, if things are as they are? The affirmation of God's present and future Kingdom therefore means the affirmation that God will act to deal with the problem, to rescue his people and complete his purpose for the whole of creation.

These two purposes (rescuing his people, completing creation) are intimately connected, as is seen in a thousand passages from Genesis to Revelation. God's call of Israel to be his people, to live under his rule, was itself designed as the central move in putting the world to rights. But Israel was itself part of the problem (being composed of sinful human beings). This generated a second-order problem, mirroring the first, as the parallel between the Babylonian exile and the expulsion from Eden bears witness. In both cases (humankind in general, Israel in particular) it is idolatry, the worship of something other than the creator God, which is identified as the central evil. Idolatry generates all kinds of less-than-truly-human ways of living, both outside and inside Israel. This produces the double problem which determines much of the Old Testament and Jewish thought, prayer, and writing: How is Israel to be rescued, and how is the whole world to be put to rights?

Without the problem of evil, there would be no need to speak of, pray for, or invoke God's Kingdom or authority; it would be apparent as a present reality. To speak of God's Kingdom is thus to invoke God as the sovereign one who has the right, the duty, and the power to deal appropriately with evil in the world, in Israel, and in human beings, and thereupon to remake the world, Israel, and human beings. This fresh, gracious, and forgiving purpose, aimed at new creation, is put into effect through the renewal of the covenant. Our question can then be sharpened up: What was, and is, the role of scripture within this divine purpose? If this is what "God's authority" looks like, what part does an authoritative scripture have within it?

When full allowance is made for the striking differences of genre and emphasis within scripture, we may propose that Israel's sacred writings were the place where, and the means by which, Israel discovered again and again who the true God was, and how his Kingdom-purposes were being taken forward. Reciting the scriptures was central to worship, not least in rehearsing God's Kingdom-revealing deeds and thus evoking praise and hope. Scripture did not just *reflect* the experience, religious awareness, social and cultural turmoils, and so forth of God's people, though of course it did all that as well. Again and again the point of scripture was that it addressed a fresh, prophetic word *to* Israel in the midst of its often very ambiguous "experience," breaking into Israel's own world of muddle and mistakes—doing, in fact, in verbal form what God himself was doing in breaking into the world, and into Israel's life, in judgment and mercy. Though it is in the prophetic books that we can see this most clearly (not least through the autobiographical passages in which the prophet's call, or struggle with God's word, stands out), a full account of the role of scripture within the life of Israel would appear as a function of Israel's election by God for the sake of the world. Through scripture, God was equipping his people to serve his purposes.

Actually, "equipping" is a somewhat inadequate shorthand for the multiple tasks scripture accomplished. Through scripture, Israel was given order in her national life, a structured worship, wisdom for the conduct of daily life, rebuke and promise through the prophets, and, not least, songs through which to bring every mood, every moment into God's presence as praise, lament, adoration, perplexity, despair, hope, and commitment. And that is to list only the most obvious features.

Inspiration and "the Word of YHWH"

This is where the notion of "inspiration" comes in. "Inspiration" is a shorthand way of talking about the belief that by his Spirit God guided the very different writers and editors, so that the books they produced were the books God intended his people to have. This is not the subject of the present book, but we should note that some kind of divine inspiration of scripture was taken for granted in most of the ancient Israelite scriptures themselves, as well as in the beliefs of the early Christians. The emergence of a "canon" of scripture, though it has been controversial in some respects in recent discussion, was at its heart an attempt to track the way in which *these* books had become formative for the life of God's people, to honor the fact that God had somehow given them to his people, and to remind Israel to honor them and attend to them appropriately. And in and through it all we find the elusive but powerful idea of God's "word," not as a synonym for the written scriptures, but as a strange personal presence, creating, judging, healing, recreating.

"By the word of YHWH were the heavens made, and all the host of them by the breath of his mouth"; "Is not my word like a fire, and like a hammer that breaks the rock in pieces?"; "All flesh is like grass; it withers and fades, but the word of our God will stand for ever"; "Like the rain and snow, coming down and watering the earth . . . so shall my word be that goes forth from my mouth; it will not return to me empty, but it will succeed in the tasks for which I send it"; "The word is near you, on your lips and in your heart, so that you may do it" (Psalm 33:6; Jeremiah 23:29; Isaiah 40:8; 55:10–11; Deuteronomy 30:14).

This view of YHWH's "word" in the Old Testament is very instructive. It is as though, to put it one way, "the word of YHWH" is like an enormous reservoir, full of creative divine wisdom and power, into which the prophets and other writers tap by God's call and grace, so that the word may flow through them to do God's work of flooding or irrigating his people. Or, to put it another way, the creator God, though utterly transcendent over and different from the world which he has made, remains present and active within that world, and one of the many ways in which this is so is through his living and active word. This reflects God's own nature on the one hand; it is a natural and normal thing for this God to speak, not some anthropomorphic projection onto a blank deistic screen! On the other hand, it reflects the fact that, within God's world, one of the most powerful things human beings, God's image-bearers, can do is to speak. Words change things—through promises, commands, apologies, warnings, declarations of love or of implacable opposition to evil. The notion of "speech-acts," which we referred to already, is fairly new in philosophy. It would not have surprised the ancient Israelite prophets. As Walter Brueggemann puts it in his *Theology of the Old Testament* (Eerdmans, 1997, 146), expounding Psalm 33:6: "The imagery is of a powerful sovereign who utters a decree from the throne, issues a fiat, and in the very utterance the thing is done."

Israel: The Scripture-Hearing People

Israel was thus constituted, from one point of view, as the people who heard God's word—in call, promise, liberation, guidance, judgment, forgiveness, further judgment, renewed liberation, and renewed promise. (That sequence is intended as a summary of the entire Old Testament narrative from Abraham to the "post-exilic" period.) This is what I mean by denying that scripture can be reduced to the notion of the "record of a revelation," in the sense of a mere writing down of earlier, and assumedly prior, "religious experience." To think like that would be to superimpose categories entirely foreign to the Old Testament's authors, editors, or hearers. We cannot reduce "thus says YHWH" to "thus says Jeremiah" without squashing our own framework on top of theirs, and indeed on their experiences as well. We have for too long been in thrall to philosophers like Feuerbach, who wanted to reduce all talk of God to talk of humans and their experiences.

Equally, scripture was never simply about the imparting of information, reminding people of a previous religious experience. Even when the biblical writers were telling the story of Israel, this was never merely in order to provide facts about the past for their own sake. The story was told in order to generate once more the sense of Israel as the people called by YHWH for his purposes in the world, so that the writing and the telling of the story formed the further living embodiment of YHWH's call and promise. It was written to shape and direct the life of God's people. The inner tensions and puzzles of the Old Testament—one thinks, for instance, of the apparent clash between Deuteronomy and Job, the one suggesting that virtue is rewarded in this life, the other hotly contesting it—reflect how many sides there are to this task, and how complex it is to recognize that Israel is *both* the bearer of God's healing promise for the world *and* itself a people who belong to the world and who stand under the same need of judgment and healing.

Our word "authority" is, frankly, far too narrowly focused to do justice to all this. To attempt to sum up the role which scripture played within Israel we would need to say something like "God's sovereign activity in, through, to and for Israel by means of his spoken and written word." Or, to put it more simply, "God's sovereignty operating through scripture." "God spoke and it was done." The word itself, as in Isaiah 40:8 and 55:11, carried power and new life.

Scripture in Second-Temple Judaism

In the second-Temple period (roughly, the last four centuries BC) we observe scripture's "authority" operating in at least two interlocking ways.

1. It formed the controlling *story* in which Israel struggled to find its identity and destiny as the covenant people through and for whom God's justice would ultimately break upon the world. This controlling story itself became controversial

in the ancient world, when different groups told Israel's story differently. This has been picked up in our own day, when some writers have pointed out the difficulty of summarizing the sprawling, awkward scriptural narratives within a single coherent storyline. This does not mean that one cannot find broad outlines of an overarching narrative within the Jewish scriptures; and the observable problems did not prevent scripture functioning in precisely this way within the Judaism of Jesus's day.

2. It formed the call to a present *obedience* (interpreted, for instance, by the early rabbis' exposition of Torah, or the early legal rulings we find in some of the texts from Qumran) through which Israel could respond appropriately to God's call. Israel would thus be modeling the genuinely human existence which God willed for the whole world by living "under" scripture as controlling narrative and guide for daily life. Scripture—read, studied, taught, prayed and sung, in the Temple, in the early synagogues, in the Qumran community, daily and weekly and at the great festivals and solemn fasts—became the key factor shaping Israel as the people who longed for the coming of the Kingdom. The multiple and widely varying types of Judaism in Jesus's day can be plotted in terms of different ways of understanding and attempting to live under scripture and thus to work, pray, and wait for God to bring the story in which they were living to its proper conclusion.

3.

Scripture and Jesus

"When the time had fully come, God sent forth his son. . . ." (Galatians 4:4). Understanding Jesus within his historical context means understanding him where, according to scripture itself, he belongs.

Jesus Accomplishes That to Which Scripture Had Pointed

A historically grounded understanding of Jesus's proclamation, achievement, death, and resurrection suggests that at the heart of his work lay the sense of bringing the *story* of scripture to its climax, and thereby offering to God the *obedience* through which the Kingdom would be accomplished. As he himself declared, "The time is fulfilled; God's kingdom is at hand." There is of course quite a lot to be said about Jesus himself, and within that about his relationship to Israel's scriptures. I have written about this at length elsewhere, and for our present purposes need only to draw out some short, but vital, points. (See, for instance, *Jesus and the Victory of God* [Fortress Press, 1996]; *The Challenge of Jesus* [Inter-Varsity Press, 1999].)

For good historical reasons, I cannot agree with those (not least some members of the "Jesus Seminar") who have suggested in the last decade or so that Jesus was either illiterate or nearly so, with little knowledge of or interest in Israel's scriptures. This is to invent a Jesus out of thin air, and non-Jewish thin air at that. Instead, I have argued in the books already mentioned, in line with a good deal of contemporary scholarship on his aims and motives, that Jesus believed himself called to undertake the task, marked out in various ways in Israel's scriptures, through which God's long-range purposes would at last be brought to fruition. As Telford Work puts it (p. 12), "Jewish biblical practice is actually *constitutive* of the human Jesus." What this means in practice is that in and through Jesus evil is confronted and judged, and forgiveness and renewal are brought to birth. The covenant is renewed; new creation is inaugurated. The work which God had done through scripture in the Old Testament is done by Jesus in his public career, his death, and resurrection, and his sending of the Spirit.

Jesus thus does, climactically and decisively, what scripture had in a sense been trying to do: bring God's fresh Kingdom-order to God's people and thence to the world. He is, in that sense as well as others, the Word made flesh. Who he was and is, and what he accomplished, are to be understood in the light of what scripture had said. He was, in himself, the "true Israel," formed by scripture, bringing the Kingdom to birth. When he spoke of the scripture needing to be fulfilled (e.g., Mark 14:49), he was not simply envisaging himself doing a few scattered and random acts which corresponded to various distant and detached prophetic sayings; he was thinking of the entire storyline at last coming to fruition, and of an entire world of hints and shadows now coming to plain statement and full light. This, I take it, is the deep meaning of say-ings like Matthew 5:17–18, where Jesus insists that he has come not to abolish the law but to fulfill it.

Beneath this again, as the earliest church came quickly to acknowledge, Jesus was the living embodiment of Israel's God, the God whose Spirit had inspired the scriptures in the first place. And if he understood his own vocation and identity in terms of scripture, the early church quickly learned to make the equation the other way as well: they read the Old Testament, both its story (including covenant, promise, warning, and so on) and its com-mands in terms of what they had discovered in Jesus. This is set out programmatically in Luke 24, as the two disciples on the road to Emmaus are treated to a lengthy exposition from "Moses, the prophets and all the scriptures," and as the risen Jesus opens the minds of the disciples to understand what the scriptures had been about all along (Luke 24:27, 44–45). But the same point, implicit or explicit, is everywhere apparent in the gospel stories.

Jesus Insists on Scripture's Authority

The backbone of many traditional arguments for the authority of scripture has been those specific sayings of Jesus which stress that he himself regarded scripture as authoritative and criticized his opponents for not doing so. Obvious passages include Jesus's splendid retort to the Sadducees, that they were wrong because they knew neither the Bible nor God's power (Matthew 22:29 and parallels); his attack on the scribes and Pharisees because they made God's word null and void through their traditions (Matthew 15:6–9, quoting Isaiah to the same effect); and the more cryptic argument that if Psalm 82 calls the ancient Israelites "gods," why should the one whom God has sent into the world not be called

God's son, which is backed up with the reminder that "scripture cannot be broken" (John 10:35). Granted that these are all somewhat ad hoc—in other words, that Jesus is not reported to have made the authority of scripture a major theme in his teaching—they are nonetheless important, revealing an underlying attitude which, after the manner of presuppositions, is brought into the light of day only when it has been implicitly questioned.

This attitude dovetails nicely into the previous point about Jesus's consciousness of bringing scripture to its long-awaited climax. In fact, these specific sayings about scriptural authority really work only within that context. Without it, we would remain puzzled: How can Jesus, in the very passage where he insists on the priority of scripture over human traditions, then declare all foods clean (Mark 7:1–23; Mark's own note in verse 19 underlines the point)? If he is insisting that not only the acts of murder, theft and adultery but also the cherishing of motivations toward those acts comes under divine prohibition, what can justify his apparently cavalier attitude to the sabbath? If the command to honor one's father and mother is to be fulfilled, why did Jesus not only ignore his own mother and brothers in favor of his followers (Mark 3:31–35) but also warn his followers that they would have to be prepared to hate their father, mother, and almost everyone else as well (Luke 14:26)? If scripture pointed to the exaltation of Israel and the consequent ingathering of the nations, why did Jesus say that when people came from east and west to sit down with Abraham in God's Kingdom, "the heirs of the kingdom" would be thrown out (Matthew 8:11–12)?

With the usual argument, which sees "scripture" simply in black and white, almost on a take-it-or-leave-it basis, it is hard to see what on earth is going on. Once we set Jesus in the context of the larger scriptural story, however, and come to grips with his sense of what exactly the new covenant would mean, and how it would both fulfill and transform the old one (a task which lies way beyond the scope of the present book), we discover a much richer, and more narratival, sense of "fulfillment," which generates that subtle and powerful view of scripture we find in the early church.

4.

The "Word of God" in the Apostolic Church

In the early church, the "word" offered both fulfillment of Old Testament promises and a call to accept the Spirit's life-changing power and authority in the present.

Apostolic Preaching of the "Word": The Jesus-Story as Fulfilling the (Old Testament) Scripture-Story

The earliest apostolic preaching was neither a standard Jewish message with Jesus added on at the end, nor a free-standing announcement of a new religion cut off from its Jewish roots, but rather the story of Jesus *understood as* the fulfillment of the Old Testament covenant narrative, and thus as the *euangelion,* the good news or "gospel"—the creative force which called the church into being and shaped its mission and life. It was this biblical story, rather than some other (that of human empire, say, or of individual spiritual self-discovery) that provided the interpretative matrix within which the accomplishment of Jesus made the sense it did.

The complex and multiple genres and themes of the Old Testament, shaping the life and thought of Israel, had raised in practical as well as theoretical terms the questions of good and evil, of Israel and the nations, of empire and resistance, and above all of the sovereignty, justice, and saving purposes of the creator and covenant God. It was these questions, raised in this scripturally shaped way, to which Jesus's Kingdom-movement, climaxing in his death and resurrection, offered the God-given answer.

When Paul says, quoting an earlier and widely used summary of the Christian message, "The Messiah died for our sins in accordance with the scriptures . . . and was raised on the third day in accordance with the scriptures" (1 Corinthians 15:3–4), he does not mean that he and his friends can find one or two proof-texts to back up their claim, but rather that these events have come as the climax to the long and winding narrative of Israel's scriptures. "The authority of the Old Testament" in the early church, at its heart, meant that what God had done in Jesus Christ was to be seen in terms of a character within a particular story, a portrait in a particular landscape, where everything in the story, or the landscape, points us to a key facet of who this central character is and what he has accomplished.

The earliest Christian oral tradition we can trace, and the earliest sermons we can reconstruct, embody what Paul called "the word," "the word of truth," or simply "the gospel" (for instance, Colossians 1:5; 1 Thessalonians 2:13). Thus, before there was any "New Testament," there was already a clear understanding in early Christianity that "the word of God," to which the apostles committed themselves when refusing to engage in extra administrative duties (Acts 6:1–4), lay at the heart of the church's mission and life. It is not difficult to summarize this "word." It was the story of Jesus (particularly his death and resurrection), told as the climax of the story of God and Israel and thus offering itself as both the true story of the world and the foundation and energizing force for the church's mission. Exactly this story, seen in exactly this (admittedly rather complex) way, is precisely what we find in the four canonical "gospels," and for that matter in at least some of the sources which may be deemed to stand behind them. This last point is controversial in the present climate of scholarship but is, I believe, defensible.

The Life-Changing Power of the "Word": Calling and Shaping the New Church

Paul expressed what the apostles all discovered: that this retelling of the ancient story, climaxing now in Jesus, carried *power*—power to change minds, hearts, and lives. "The gospel is God's power to salvation" (Romans 1:16; compare 1 Thessalonians 1:5; 2:13). The "word" did not "offer itself" in a take-it-or-leave-it fashion, any more than Caesar's heralds would have said, "If you'd like a new kind of imperial experience, you might like to try giving allegiance to the new emperor." The word was announced as a sovereign summons, and it brought into being a new situation, new possibilities, and a new life-changing power. The apostles and evangelists believed that the power thus unleashed was God's own power, at work through the freshly outpoured Spirit, calling into being the new covenant people, the restored Israel-for-the-world. The "word" was not just *information* about the Kingdom and its effects, important though that was and is. It was the way God's Kingdom, accomplished in Jesus, was making its way in the world (referred to in this fashion frequently in Acts—e.g., 6:7). The Kingdom, we remind ourselves, was always about the creator God acting sovereignly to put the world to rights, judging evil and bringing forgiveness and new life. This was what the "word" accomplished in those who heard it in faith and obedience.

Here we have the roots of a fully Christian theology of scriptural authority: planted firmly in the soil of the missionary community, confronting the powers of the world with the news of the Kingdom of God, refreshed and invigorated by the Spirit, growing particularly through the preaching and teaching of the apostles, and bearing fruit in the transformation of human lives as the start of God's project to put the whole cosmos to rights. God accomplishes these things, so the early church believed, through the "word": the story of Israel now told as reaching its climax in Jesus, God's call to Israel now transmuted into God's call to his renewed people. And it was this "word" which came, through the work of the early writers, to be expressed in writing in the New Testament as we know it.

The church was thus from the very beginning characterized precisely as the transformed people of God, as the community created by God's call and promise, and summoned to hear the "word" of the gospel in all its fullness. The earliest church was centrally constituted as the people called into existence, and sustained in that existence, by the powerful, effective, and (in that sense and many others) "authoritative" word of God, written in the Old Testament, embodied in Jesus, announced to the world, taught in the church. This was the heart of the church's mission (Israel's story has been fulfilled; the world must therefore hear of it); of its common life (the first "mark of the church" in Acts 2:42 is "the teaching of the apostles"); and of the call to a holiness which would express both the true Israel and the newly human dimensions ("renewed according to God's image") characteristic of the new identity. Some of the major disputes in the early church were precisely about what this holiness meant in practice.

The "Word" as Vehicle of the Spirit's Authority: Energizing, Shaping, and Directing the Church

At least one of the actual apostles (Paul), and some of their colleagues and immediate successors, wrote books which were intended to continue this work on a wider scale. Recent study of the letters, and of the intention of the gospel writers, emphasizes the self-conscious way in which the New Testament authors believed themselves called to exercise their calling as "authorized" teachers, by the guidance and power of the Spirit, writing books and letters to sustain, energize, shape, judge, and renew the church. The apostolic writings, like the "word" which they now wrote down, were not simply *about* the coming of God's Kingdom into all the world; they were, and were designed to be, part of the *means whereby that happened,* and whereby those through whom it happened could themselves be transformed into Christ's likeness.

Those who read these writings discovered, from very early on, that the books themselves carried the same power, the same *authority in action,* that had characterized the initial preaching of the "word." It used to be said that the New Testament writers "didn't think they were writing 'scripture.'" That is hard to sustain historically today. The fact that their writings were, in various senses, "occasional" (Paul's letters written to address sudden emergencies being the most striking example) is not to the point. At precisely those points of urgent need (when, for instance, writing Galatians or 2 Corinthians) Paul is most conscious that he is writing as one authorized, by the apostolic call he had received from Jesus Christ, and in the power of the Spirit, to bring life and order to the church by his words. How much more, one who begins a book with the earth-shatteringly simple "In the beginning was the word . . . and the word became flesh," and concludes it by telling his readers that "these things are written so that you may believe that the Messiah, the Son of God, is Jesus, and that by believing you may have life in his name" (John 1:1, 14; 20:31).

This is not to say, of course, that the writers of the New Testament specifically envisaged a time when their books would be collected together and form something like what we now know as the canon. I doubt very much if such an idea ever crossed their minds. But that they were conscious of a unique vocation to write Jesus-shaped, Spirit-led, church-shaping books, as part of their strange first-generation calling, we should not doubt.

The New Testament Canon: Richly Diverse or Contradictory?

This does not mean, of course, that all the early Christian writers said exactly the same thing. Few today would deny the rich diversity of their work. Yet, as we shall see presently, many of the accusations not merely of diversity but of flat contradiction arise not from historical study proper but from the imposition on the texts of categories from much later Western thought (from, for instance, the sixteenth or the nineteenth century). Obvious examples include the idea that a book which teaches "justification by faith" cannot also teach "final judgment according to works," let alone what we today see as a "high view of the church"; or that the proclamation of Jesus as "Messiah" (a Jewish category) is somehow in tension with announcing him as "Lord" (a Gentile category, supposedly). Such judgments have led many in the last two hundred years to rush to hasty conclusions about contradictions within the New Testament; but just because some Western theologians cannot see how certain categories fit coherently together, that doesn't mean that those categories didn't fit in the first century. A good many well-known apparent problems of inner-canonical coherence and complementarity are of this type. Those that remain are best seen as a challenge to further thought rather than as an undermining of the remarkably consistent proclamation of the New Testament (see chapters 4 and 5).

The Early Christian Reading of the Old Testament: God's New Covenant People and Their Place in the Ongoing Story

In particular, precisely because of what the early Christians believed about Israel's story having come to fulfillment in Jesus, they developed a *multilayered, nuanced, and theologically grounded* reading of the Old Testament. They firmly believed that the Old Testament was, and remained, the book which God had given to his people—the covenant people who had spearheaded God's purposes for the world and from whom the Messiah, Jesus, had come. But from the very beginning they read the ancient scriptures in a new way. This new way resulted in their recognizing that some parts of the scriptures were no longer relevant for their ongoing life—not, we must stress, because those parts were bad, or not God-given, or less inspired, but *because they belonged with earlier parts of the story which had now reached its climax.*

This is the key insight which enables us to understand how the early Christians understood the Old Testament and how the New Testament writers used it. Again and again one hears accusations that the New Testament writers (and their predecessors within oral teaching and tradition) treated the Old Testament as a rag-bag from which they could pick and choose what they wanted and leave what was inconvenient. This has then been used, over and over within recent decades, as an argument for saying that we today can and should treat the New Testament itself (let alone the Old Testament!) in the same way. But this is unwarranted, and springs from a misunderstanding about how the early Christians understood and used scripture.

As the renewed-Israel people, now transformed through Jesus and the Spirit into a multi-ethnic, non-geographically-based people charged with a mission to the whole world, the early Christians figured out very early on an appropriate, and in no way arbitrary, continuity and discontinuity between the Old Testament period and their own. (This has nothing in common, by the way, with the fanciful speculations and periodizations of "Dispensationalism.") This needs to be explored in more detail.

Continuity and Discontinuity in the Early Church's Use of Scripture

The earliest Christians were quickly forced into thinking through the question of continuity and discontinuity. The early controversy about the admission of non-Jews into God's people (Did they need to be circumcised? Did they need to obey the Jewish food laws and sabbath regulations?) precipitated a detailed argument, articulated by Paul in Galatians 2 and 3, about the way in which, precisely because God was fulfilling the covenant promises to Abraham by creating a single multi-ethnic family, those regulations in the Mosaic law which explicitly marked out Jews from their non-Jewish neighbors were now to be set aside, not because they were not good, or not given by God, but because they had been given for a temporary purpose which was now complete. The same pattern is repeated in many other cases. The inauguration of the new covenant in Jesus and by the Spirit meant that Christians had to work out in what sense this was the renewal of the same covenant, and in what sense it was "new" in the sense of "different." Paul himself sums up the hermeneutical tension which covenant renewal has set up: God's righteousness is revealed "apart from the Law," although "the Law and the Prophets bear witness to it" (Romans 3:21).

This provides a model which helps us to track the continuity and discontinuity which the early Christians saw between their own time and that of Israel BC. Continuity is seen, for example, in the early Christian insistence on the world as God's good creation; on God's sovereign duty and promise to deal with evil; on the covenant with Abraham as the framework by which God would achieve this universal aim; and on the call to holiness, to genuine and renewed humanness, over against the dehumanized world of pagan idolatry and immorality (though of course many in the first century saw that "holiness" as requiring adherence to the Jewish law, at which point it would tip over into the next category).

Obvious examples of discontinuity are all over the place. The ancient Jewish purity laws are seen as no longer relevant to a community in which Gentiles are welcome on equal terms (Mark 7; Acts 15; Galatians 2). The Temple in Jerusalem, and the sacrifices that took place there, are no longer the focal point of God's meeting with his people (Mark 12:28–34; Acts 7; Romans 12:1–2; Hebrews 8—10); indeed, there will be no Temple in the New Jerusalem (Revelation 21—22, the more remarkable since that passage is built on the Temple-centered climax of Ezekiel). The sabbath is no longer mandatory (Romans 14:5–6), and indeed if people insist on such observances they are cutting against the grain of the gospel (Galatians 4:10). There is now no holy land: in Paul's reinterpretation of the Abrahamic promises in Romans 4:13, God promises Abraham not just one strip of territory but the whole world, anticipating the renewal of all creation as in Romans 8. Perhaps most important, the dividing wall between Jew and Gentile has been abolished (throughout Paul, and summarized in Ephesians 2:11–22). These conclusions were reached by the early Christians, not by a cavalier process of setting aside bits of the Old Testament which they found unwelcome, but through a deep-rooted sense, worked out theologically and practically, that all of that scripture had been summed up in Jesus Christ (Matthew 5:17, itself summing up the message of much of the book; Romans 3:31; 2 Corinthians 1:20) and that now God's project of new covenant and new creation had begun, necessarily taking a new mode. John sums it up in a sentence which has often teased commentators. "The law," he writes, "was given through Moses; grace and truth came through Jesus Christ" (1:17). Should we understand him to mean "*but* grace and truth came through Jesus Christ," or should it be "*and*"? The rest of the gospel suggests that John deliberately left it ambiguous.

The early Christian use of the Old Testament reflects exactly this double-edged position. Precisely because of the emphasis on the unique accomplishment of Jesus Christ, the Old Testament could not continue to have exactly the same role within the Christian community that it had had before. Christianity does not *repeat* the earlier stages of the story, any more than it repeats the unique achievement of Jesus; it celebrates and builds upon them. From the start, in the ministry of Jesus and the work of Paul, we find constant reference to the fact that with the fulfillment comes a new moment in the story, a new act in the play (see pages 121–127). Heavy-handed schemes such as those of Marcion (the God of the Old Testament is a different God to that of the New) and the theologically cognate ones of some Reformers (a strict antithesis between law and gospel pressed into meaning that, as Luther once said despite his general awareness that things were not quite so simple, "Moses knows nothing of Christ") do no justice to the sophisticated early Christian sense of continuing to live under the *whole* scripture, albeit in this *multilayered* manner. Nor, for that matter, do the pragmatic, rule-of-thumb conclusions of some other writers of the sixteenth and seventeenth centuries, who saw the "civil" and "ceremonial" laws being abolished while the "moral" ones remained, ignoring the fact that most ancient Jews would not have recognized such a distinction.

It is not hard to imagine illustrations of how this continuity and discontinuity function. When travelers sail across a vast ocean and finally arrive on the distant shore, they leave the ship behind and continue over land, not because the ship was no good, or because their voyage had been misguided, but precisely because both ship and voyage had accomplished their purpose. During the new, dry-land stage of their journey, the travelers remain—and in this illustration must never forget that they remain—the people who made that voyage in that ship.

Perhaps the best example of this line of thought anywhere in the New Testament is one of the earliest: Galatians 3:22–29, where Paul argues that God gave the Mosaic law for a specific purpose which has now come to fruition, whereupon that law must be put aside, in terms of its task of defining the community, not because it was a bad thing but because it was a good thing whose task is now accomplished. But, as the whole letter indicates, the people of God renewed through Jesus and the Spirit can never and must never forget the road by which they had traveled.

The New Testament in Dialogical Relation with All Human Culture

The New Testament emerged, then, as the written expression of that word under which the earliest Christians knew themselves to be living—indeed, *by* which they found life in all its fullness. It was assumed from the start that this word had broken in, and would continue to break in, to human life, culture, aspirations and assumptions. The written word, expressing and embodying the living word of the primitive gospel, was the Spirit-empowered agent through which the one creator God was reclaiming the cosmos, and as such it offered the way to a truly human life; but it stood sharply over against some understandings of what a truly human life might be. It was the way to the fulfillment of God's plan for Israel; but it stood over against other interpretations which failed to recognize Jesus as Messiah. Like Jesus's parables themselves, the emerging early Christian writings both reaffirmed and redefined existing perceptions of what the important questions really were and what the true answers might be.

All this means, significantly, that one can never assume that any part of a culture, ancient or modern, is automatically to be endorsed or rejected. There was much in the Jewish world which was endorsed as it stood within early Christianity, and much which, for good theological reasons, was set aside. Equally, there was much in the non-Jewish world which the early Christians were able to use. Paul speaks of "taking every thought captive to obey Christ" (2 Corinthians 10:4), and he can assume a deep commonality between the world's perceptions of "good" and "evil" and those to which the Christian church must adhere (Romans 12:9, 17; Philippians 4:8). But there was much against which the church found itself compelled to stand out, no matter how deep-rooted— identifying, even!—it was within the local culture. Think of the goddess Diana at Ephesus, and the riot which Paul faced there. The "word," spoken and written, always summoned people to a costly and contested redemption and renewal through dying and rising with Christ in baptism and the struggle to live on that basis, to reflect the image of the creator God. Again and again it was the apostolic proclamation, eventually coming to expression in the New Testament writings, which guided the early church in discerning the relationship between cultural context and the path of new, renewed humanity.

This has nothing to do with the declaration of an arbitrary or "controlling" ethic, a standard imposed from without by constricting or bullying authority in the early church. It has everything to do with understanding human renewal as the beginning, the pointer toward, and even the means of, God's eventual eradication of evil from the world and the bringing to birth of the new creation itself. Thus, so the early Christians believed, God's word was at work by the Spirit within the community, to put Jesus's achievement into effect and thus to advance the final Kingdom. We can summarize it like this: the New Testament understands itself as the new covenant charter, the book that forms the basis for the new telling of the story through which Christians are formed, reformed and transformed so as to be God's people for God's world. That is the challenge the early Christians bequeath to us as we reconsider what "the authority of scripture" might mean in practice today.

5.

The First Sixteen Centuries

We must now compress a very long and complicated story—the story of how the church lived with scripture for sixteen hundred years—into a very short account, highlighting only those things which appear immediately relevant to our present study.

Meeting Early Challenges to Scripture with an Appeal to Scripture Itself, to Early Tradition, and to Good Exegesis

Close to the heart of Christianity in the second and third centuries was the sense of the church as the community that lives with and under scripture. Scripture furnished the church with the wherewithal for the proclamation and living of the Kingdom. It sustained the church in prayer and holiness. It enabled the early Christians to respond to questions and attacks. The challenge of Marcion and the Gnostics to a radical reconfiguration (and at least a semi-paganization) of Christianity was met with a fresh appeal to scripture itself, with the claim that the church had always understood things this way (at this point we see the development of the early "rule of faith"), and with detailed arguments (for instance, those of Irenaeus against the Gnostics) about the actual meaning of specific contested passages.

Thus was born the church's characteristic account of itself to outsiders, and its characteristic exploration of its own riches: appeal to scripture as central, backed up by an account of previous understandings ("tradition") and by a thought-out exposition, integrated in various ways with, and also standing over against, leading ideas of the day (Justin, Tertullian, etc.), which we might, with only slight anachronism, label "reason" (see pages 120–121). Scripture remained central; indeed, sermons based on scripture, and commentaries which expounded it in detail, were at the heart of the normal theological life of the church in the early centuries. The study of the early church as the scripture-reading community is one of the best ways of getting right to the heart of what early Christianity was all about.

Reaffirming the Scriptural Narrative Against the "Newly" Discovered Alternative Christianities

The appeal to scripture was above all an appeal, at a structural as well as detailed level, to what may be called a *renewed-Jewish* view of God, the world and humankind. This can be demonstrated in thousands of detailed statements. To stay at a broad general level, the claim to be a people rooted in Israel's story and recreated through the death and resurrection of Israel's Messiah, and thus to be living out the vocation to be genuine human beings, safeguarded *creational and covenantal monotheism* over against, first, the essentially platonic dualism of the Gnostics and others, and second, the omnipresent paganism of the Greco-Roman world.

(More details on this rather dense theological statement can be found in Chapter 9 of my book *The New Testament and the People of God*.)

The irony of claiming this renewed-Jewish status, while following a Messiah most Jews still regarded as an impostor, emerges in the line of thought extending from Paul (e.g., in Romans 9–11) to Justin's *Dialogue with Trypho* and beyond. But the existence of this tension only reminds us of what was at stake in the church's living with scripture and its refusal to abandon it in favor of the very different theological stance of, for instance, the so-called "Gospel of Thomas." The claim of writers like Justin, Tertullian, and Irenaeus, and their scriptural basis and appeal, led to the emphasis on the *historical* nature of the church, with its stress on continuity from Jesus's day to their own, and indeed on the continuity of the people of Abraham, transformed through Jesus the Messiah but still obedient to the same world-transforming call.

Recent writings have subjected this claim to fresh versions of familiar challenges. Part of the recent energy for discovering "alternative" modes of early Christianity, and for suggesting that other texts were "excluded" from the mainstream in the interests of squelching vibrant forms of early Christian living, comes from a late-Protestant alarm at such an apparently "early-Catholic" position, and partly from the late-modern eagerness for religions of "self-discovery" over against those of redemption. Such positions (both scholarly and popular; the enormous appeal of the wildly fanciful novel *The Da Vinci Code* is to be understood in the same way as the fondness of scholars for "discovering" that some Coptic or Syriac text has revealed what Jesus "really" thought) gain their force from an appeal to a general sense within late-modern Western culture, particularly in the United States, that orthodox Christianity has been demonstrated to be bad for individuals and societies, and that its oppressive nature, colluding with enslaving forces, was already emerging in the writing and privileging of the biblical canon as we know it. People sometimes suggest, indeed, that the process of canonization is the sign that the church itself was the final authority. This proposal is sometimes made by Catholic traditionalists asserting the supremacy of the church over the Bible, and sometimes by postmodern skeptics asserting that the canon itself, and hence the books included in it, were all part of a power play for control within the church and social respectability in the world. This makes a rather obvious logical mistake analogous to that of a soldier who, receiving orders through the mail, concludes that the letter carrier is his commanding officer. Those who transmit, collect and distribute the message are not in the same league as those who write it in the first place.

Such proposals have, in fact, little to recommend them historically, despite enthusiastic advocacy in some quarters. They represent, among other things, a serious de-Judaizing of the Christian tradition. The canonization of scripture, both Jewish and Christian, was no doubt complicated by all kinds of less-than-perfect human motivations, as indeed in the writing of scripture in the first place. But canonization was never simply a matter of a choice of particular books on a "who's in, who's out" basis. It was a matter of setting out the larger story, the narrative framework, which makes sense of and brings order to God's world and God's people.

We should note, as of some importance in the early history of the Bible-reading church, that those who were being burned alive, thrown to the lions, or otherwise persecuted, tortured and killed were normally those who were reading Matthew, Mark, Luke, John, Paul, and the rest. The kind of spirituality generated by "Thomas" and similar books would not have worried the Roman imperial authorities, for reasons not unconnected with the fact that

"Thomas" and the similar collections of sayings are non-narratival, deliberately avoiding the option of placing the sayings within the overarching framework of the story of Israel. It is sometimes said or implied that the canonical books, unlike those found in other collections, were written as a way of making early Christianity more socially and culturally respectable. Irenaeus, who returned to Lyons as bishop after his predecessor had been martyred along with several other Christians in 177, and who remained an implacable opponent of the kind of theology found in "Thomas" and similar writings and an enthusiastic supporter and expositor of scripture, would have found such a proposal grimly amusing. As his writings make abundantly clear, it was the canonical scriptures that sustained the early church in its energetic mission and its commitment, startling to the watching pagan world, to a radical holiness.

A Diminishing Focus on the Narrative Character and Israel-Dimension of Scripture

The church's hold on the Jewish sense of the scriptural story was hard to maintain. Over the next few centuries, with the gradual loss of the Israel-dimension in the church's understanding of itself and its scriptures, the notion of scriptural authority became detached from its narrative context, and thereby isolated from both the gift and the goal of the Kingdom. As Telford Work has demonstrated, many theologians, not least Augustine, remained passionately committed to God's work through scripture in bringing people to faith, to holiness and to salvation. But we miss, in some of the developing tradition, the dynamic notion of scripture as the vehicle of God's Kingdom coming to birth in the world. The notion of "authority" which we have sketched in terms of "God at work powerfully through scripture to bring about the

Kingdom, by calling and shaping a new covenant people and equipping its leaders to be teachers and preachers," became gradually flattened out into two things in particular. First, scripture came to be regarded as a "court of appeal," the source-book or rule-book from which doctrine and ethics might be deduced and against which innovations were to be judged. Second, scripture was used for *lectio divina,* the practice in which individual readers could hear God speaking to them personally, nourishing their own spirituality and devotion.

"Allegorical" Exegesis as a (Flawed) Sign of the Church's Commitment to Stick with Scripture

From at least Origen (ca. 185–254) onward, some Christian theologians used allegory as a major technique for understanding the Bible. At its heart, allegory (already extensively employed by the first-century Jewish philosopher and statesman Philo, who like Origen lived in Alexandria) reads the surface text as a code through which hidden meanings may be discerned. It is partially anticipated in at least some of Jesus's parables, though the extent to which Jesus himself intended the details of his stories to be pressed into such use continues to be debated. The apocalyptic scenes in Daniel and other books of the Old Testament are explained allegorically within the texts themselves. Paul uses explicit allegorical exegesis of the Old Testament in Galatians 4:21–31; so does 1 Peter 3:20–22. Perhaps the best-known example of subsequent allegorical reading of scripture is the use of the spectacular erotic love-poem we know as the Song of Songs as an allegory of the love between Christ and the church, in parallel with Jewish readings about the love between YHWH and Israel.

What the use of allegory highlights, of course, is the church's insistence on the importance of continuing to live with scripture, the whole scripture, including the bits which appeared deeply problematic—for instance, some of the more shocking stories in the Old Testament. This is where we see a tension developing between authority and interpretation: How far can a reinterpretation of the text go before it ceases to carry the authority which was the point of interpreting it in the first place? At what point in this process are we forced to conclude that what is *really* "authoritative" within such an operation is the system of theology or devotion already believed or embraced on other grounds, which is then "discovered" in the text by the interpretative method being used?

I suspect that the New Testament writers, faced with the later allegorizers, would want to ask them certain questions. Why did they find those texts problematic? Did they not realize that the Bible is more than simply a repository of moral examples and dogmatic teaching? Could they not see that scripture offers itself, as a whole and in many of its parts, as a narrative in which, in many cases at least, human wickedness is allowed to be seen as what it is in order that God's dealings with Israel may be properly understood? Thus, for instance, Judah's conviction of incest with Tamar (Genesis 38) is the missing link between his arrogant behavior in 37:26, proposing to sell Joseph into slavery, and his humble volunteering to be Joseph's slave in place of Benjamin (44:18–34). The horrible tale of the Levite's concubine in Judges 19 was never intended as any kind of moral example; it was part of the writer's repeated argument about how chaotic life is when there is no king. David's adultery with Bathsheba (2 Samuel 11) sets the tone in court which is followed by Amnon's rape of the other Tamar (2 Samuel 13), which in turn precipitates Absalom's rebellion and David's disgrace (2 Samuel 15). These passages, though hardly "improving stories" in the sense of cozy moral tales, nevertheless do not need in fact to be read allegorically in order for their powerful theological point to emerge. And, at a second-order level, why did the allegorizers not pick up the New Testament's own nuanced and layered understanding of the ways in which the Christian reading of the Old Testament involved both continuity and discontinuity?

Allegorization, then, represents both an insistence that the church must go on living with and under scripture and a failure, at some levels at least, to understand how scripture itself actually works. Granted, there are different types of allegory, and different reasons for undertaking allegorical exegesis—complexities which would take us too far afield in this book. But it looks as though at least some uses of allegory constitute a step away from the Jewish world of the first century within which Jesus and his first followers were at home. Allegory was in one sense, as is sometimes claimed, a way of "saving the Bible for the church," in the sense that with the other reading strategies available at the time the less savory passages of the Old Testament might have been jettisoned altogether. And of course the allegorical readers always conducted their exegesis within the framework of the early Christian rule of faith, which gave their thinking a Christian narrative shape. But allegorical exegesis always ran the risk of conceding a great deal at a more fundamental level by encouraging people to see the Bible in a de-storied and hence de-Judaized way. At this level, allegory was one symptom of a move away from the primacy of the scriptural narrative itself, foreshadowing those attempts in our own day to live under scripture which are in fact an appeal, not to the Bible itself, but to a particular tradition within the life of the church.

The Medieval "Four Senses": Another (Flawed) Attempt to Get at the Rich Contours of Scripture

The allegorical exegesis offered by some of the early interpreters was continued and developed in a highly refined and imaginative way through the medieval period. Theologians came to distinguish four different senses of scripture: the literal, the allegorical, the anagogical, and the moral.

By the "literal" sense they meant the original meaning—which, confusingly, might itself include allegory, as in Paul's interpretation of the story of Sarah and Hagar in Galatians 4, or metaphor, as in Jesus's saying, "I am the good shepherd." (We should note that this is a different meaning of "literal" than some later ones; see pages 73–74.) The "allegorical" sense was the discovery of Christian doctrine within a passage whose original meaning did not seem to have anything to do with it: thus, for instance, Abraham's sending of his servant to find a bride for his son (Genesis 24) could be read as an allegory of God sending the gospel, and/or the Spirit, and/or an evangelist, to find a bride (i.e., the church) for his son (i.e., Jesus Christ). The "anagogical" sense was a way of discovering in the text a picture of the future life. Perhaps the best-known (and still frequently instinctively understood) example of this would be the use of Psalms that speak of going up to Jerusalem as a way of referring to the Christian's destination in the heavenly city. ("Anagogical" means "leading upward"—i.e., lifting up the mind and heart to contemplate the things above, as in Colossians 3:1–2.) The "moral" sense was a way of discovering lessons on how to behave hidden within texts which were not straightforwardly teaching such a thing.

As with the earlier allegorization of writers like Origen, the main thing to note about such complexities of method is that they represent ways of ensuring that, even if scripture seemed opaque, it was the church's duty and calling to live by and under it. Once more, it was a way of reading scripture within the rule of faith, a way of insisting on the authority of scripture even while, from some perspectives at least, failing to pay attention to what scripture itself was saying. However, we should not miss the point that is often made today about the medieval worldview. We who live on the near side of the Enlightenment and all its scientific revolutions have inherited a sense of a disconnected and fragmented world, and are having to learn with great difficulty—for instance, in our ecological care of the planet—that things are more interconnected than they had seemed. The medieval mind characteristically took it for granted that everything, in all spheres of divine and human affairs, in every part of the created order, was connected in a wonderful and complex web within which one might travel in thought from one part to another, observing harmony at every point. The four senses of scripture, which seem so arbitrary to the modern world (for all that we have sometimes reinvented them under other guises, as in the effort of modern redaction-criticism to get away from the literal meaning of the gospels and to discern several different layers of symbolic meanings in their plot, characterization, geography, and so on), drew on this sense of interconnectedness to suggest, in effect, that wherever one opened the Bible one might discover not only what happened in the past, but an open door upon the riches of Christian truth, the glory that lay ahead and the solid ground of Christian morality. This was a laudable aim, replicating by another means some aspects at least of what can be obtained by the kind of reading for which the present book is arguing.

Not without a cost, however. As even apologists for the medieval period will admit, once allegory had taken over, almost anything could be "proved" from scripture, resulting in fantastic and highly speculative theories. Sometimes these are simply flights of fancy, as when the twelfth-century Hugh of St. Victor suggested that Noah's Ark, being three hundred cubits long, pointed to the cross—since the Greek letter T, in the shape of a cross, represents the number three hundred. (This was part of the medieval determination to see every aspect of the Noah story as a foreshadowing of events in the life of Jesus, in line with the hint in 1 Peter 3:20–22; famously, even Noah's drunkenness was included, and became the subject of many great paintings.)

The trouble with all this is of course the lack of control. Once you can make scripture stand on its hind legs and dance a jig, it becomes a tame pet rather than a roaring lion. It is no longer "authoritative" in any strict sense; that is, it may be cited as though in "proof" of some point or other, but it is not leading the way, energizing the church with the fresh breath of God himself. The question must always be asked, whether scripture is being used to serve an existing theology or vice versa. Concerns like this contributed to the complex set of circumstances which generated the sixteenth-century Reformation.

The Development of "Tradition"

The popularity of the "four senses" went hand in hand with an increased insistence on the parallel authority, alongside scripture, of "tradition"—and hence, of course, of the church as the guardian and developer of that tradition. Whereas for Thomas Aquinas the definition of "tradition" had been, more or less, "what the church has said as it has expounded scripture," by the sixteenth century a position had been reached which regarded "tradition" as the essential supplement to, and indeed interpretative framework for, the

Bible. (This development is in some ways at least parallel to the Jewish idea of the "unwritten Torah" which, along with the "written Torah," was supposedly given by God to Moses on Mount Sinai.) This meant that anything which could be regarded as well established in ecclesial tradition, even if there was nothing about it in the Bible, and even if it appeared to go against some of the things which the Bible itself said, could be taught as authoritative and backed up with clever allegorical exegesis. (The perpetual virginity of Mary would be a good example.) The status of tradition, and its relation to scripture, has remained a matter of controversy to this day, not only between Roman Catholics and Protestants, but also within Roman Catholicism itself.

Sola Scriptura and the Reformation

The Reformers' *sola scriptura* slogan was part of their protest against perceived medieval corruptions. Go back to scripture, they insisted, and you will find the once-for-all death of Jesus but not the Mass, justification by faith but not purgatory, the power of God's word but not that of the pope. Their insistence that scripture contains all things necessary to salvation (a point which remains loud and clear in the formularies of most of the churches which take their origins from the Reformation) was part of their protest against the Roman insistence on belief in dogmas like transubstantiation as necessary articles of faith. It was never a way of saying that one had to believe every single thing in the scriptures in order to be saved. Rather, it provided, on the one hand, a statute of limitations: nothing *beyond* scripture is to be taught as needing to be believed in order for one to be saved. On the other hand, it gave a basic signpost on the way: the great truths taught in scripture are indeed the way of salvation, and those entrusted with the teaching office in the church have no right to use that office to teach anything else.

The Reformers thus set scripture over against the traditions of the church; the recovery of the literal sense over against the lush growth of the three other senses; and the right of ordinary Christians to read scripture for themselves over against the protection of the sacred text by the Latin-reading elite. They did so in order to insist that the church had gotten off the right track and that the living God was using scripture itself to get it back on the right one. Scripture was not just a resource to be brought in to back up, or to knock down, a particular idea. When expounded faithfully, with proper attention given to the central New Testament emphasis on the cross and resurrection of Jesus Christ as the turning-point of all history—it happened once and once only, they stressed, and could not be repeated with each Mass—God's word would once again do a fresh work in the hearts and lives of ordinary people. It was with these ordinary people in mind that some of the great Reformers became translators, the best known being Luther in Germany and Tyndale in England. Both men exercised a lasting influence, not only on Christian thinking but on the languages of their people in the subsequent centuries.

The "Literal Sense" at the Reformation

It is important to notice a key difference in meaning between one of the Reformers' central technical terms and the way in which the same word has been used in the modern period. When the Reformers insisted on the "literal" sense of scripture, they were referring to the first of the four medieval senses. Though, as we saw, this would often refer to the historical meaning and referent of scripture (when scripture says that Solomon's men built the Temple, for example, the literal sense is that Solomon's men built the Temple), the "literal" sense actually means "the sense of the letter"; and if the "letter"—the actual words used by the original authors or editors—is metaphorical, so be it. Thus, confusingly for us perhaps, the "literal" sense of Psalm 18:8, which speaks of smoke coming out of God's nostrils, is that, by this rich metaphor, the Psalmist is evoking the active and terrifying indignation of the living God against those who oppress his people.

The Reformers were careful to explain this point when arguing for what they saw as the metaphorical sense of Jesus's words at the Last Supper ("This is my body") over against what to us would be called the "literal" sense—i.e., the view that (as we say) Jesus "meant it literally," which would support a rather crude notion of transubstantiation. For them, the "literal" sense was *the sense that the first writers intended,* which in this case, they argued, was some kind of figurative meaning. That particular dispute aside, we need to note carefully that to invoke "the literal meaning of scripture," hoping thereby to settle a point by echoing the phraseology of the Reformers, could be valid only if we meant, not "literal" *as opposed to metaphorical,* but "literal" (which might include metaphorical if that, arguably, was the original sense) as opposed to the three other medieval senses (allegorical, anagogical, and/or moral). This is one of those many points at which the later appeal to the rhetoric of the Reformation needs to be scrutinized rather carefully. Today, when people say "literalist," they often mean "fundamentalist." The Reformers' stress on the literal sense by no means supports the kind of position thereby implied. To this we shall return.

The Reformers and "Tradition"

Although the Reformers refused to regard non-biblical tradition as a *separate* authoritative source (and liked to quote passages like Mark 7:8, where Jesus castigates the scribes and Pharisees for placing human tradition over against divine command), they regularly appealed to the church fathers, demonstrating their own continuity with earlier, premedieval times and interpretations. They were, after all, uncomfortably aware of the charge of mere innovation; the church had been there for fifteen hundred years, declared their opponents, and where had they been all that time? They, like Irenaeus against the Gnostics, went back again and again to lexically based historical exegesis—many of the Reformers, especially John Calvin, were outstanding biblical commentators—over against subtle and fanciful readings generated from within (and in turn sustaining) a different worldview, that of the medieval church. But it is arguable that the Reformers never advanced a long way beyond the impasse implied in the polarizing of scripture and tradition. They wanted to insist that they stood in line with the best of what had gone before, but never developed ways of explaining how that totality, the combination of scripture and the history of what the church had said as it read scripture, might fit together.

Scripture and Tradition in the Counter-Reformation

When the Council of Trent, called by Rome to answer the Reformers' charges and proposals, went to work on the question of scripture and tradition, it came up with formulae which remain part of Roman Catholic doctrine and catechesis to this day.

Scripture and tradition, declared Trent (Session 4.8; 8 April 1546), were to be received as of equal authority. The Second Vatican Council, four hundred years later, stated that scripture and tradition "flow from the same divine wellspring, merge into a unity and move toward the same goal." It has always been the Protestant position that scripture must remain as the test of which traditions are genuine and true interpretations of scripture (this is what, for example, virtually all churches believe in the case of the Nicene Creed) and which ones represent distortions and corruptions. This debate continues.

For our present purposes, which are to clarify and expound the way in which scripture can be authoritative, we should note that as soon as we start talking about "scripture and tradition" as two *sources of authority* we are in fact using the word "authority" itself in a subtly different way. If a man refers to two women as "my two wives," implying that he is simultaneously married to both, the word *wife* itself has changed its meaning. In the case of "authority," the idea of two parallel streams indicates that, rather than moving toward something like the dynamic concept we are expounding, both the Reformers and their opponents were understanding "authority" primarily in terms of "the place where you could go to find an authoritative ruling." This was quite natural, seeing that this was one of the main meanings of "authority" at that time. But it does not help us very much in addressing the questions we have raised in this book, which have to do with the way in which scripture carries the dynamic, saving power of God.

The Reformers and the Story of God

What we miss today, as we read the Reformers, is something which is vital within scripture itself but which, in their attention to the details, they were not concerned to stress: the great *narrative* of God, Israel, Jesus, and the world, coming forward into our own day and looking ahead to the eventual renewal of all things. True, their insistence on the once-for-all nature of Jesus's sacrificial death is rooted in what today we would call a sense of "eschatology," an awareness that the single great narrative of God and the world turned its unique corner at that point and, having done so, could not be thought to do so again without undermining the original claim. (If you were asked to sign a contract for a second time, you would assume that there was something wrong with the first one.) But the Reformers do not seem to have gone very far toward allowing this genuinely biblical insight to work its way through into that powerful sense of an ongoing narrative, into which we ourselves are enfolded at a later stage, for which I and others are now arguing.

Thus, for instance, their readings of the gospels show little awareness of them as anything other than repositories of dominical teaching, concluding with the saving events of Good Friday and Easter but without integrating those events into the Kingdom-proclamation that preceded them. This weakness is understandable in that, in their desire to break with the immediate past in order to return to that of a thousand years before, they were unlikely to want to give houseroom to much sense of historical continuity within church history as a whole.

But the main point to note from this glance at the sixteenth century is that the Reformers' insistence on the authority of scripture made several important points, but left many other matters open for further discussion. Of one thing we may be absolutely sure. If the Reformers could return and address us today, they would not say, "We got it all right; you must follow our exegesis and theology and implement it precisely as it stands." What they would say

is, "You must follow our *method:* read and study scripture for all
it's worth, and let it do its work in the world, in and through you
and your churches." They would not be surprised if, as a result,
we came up at some points with different, or differently nuanced,
theological and practical proposals. They would encourage us to
go where scripture led, using all the tools available to us, and being
prepared to challenge all human traditions, including the "Reformation" traditions themselves, insofar as scripture itself encouraged
us to do so.

The Place of "Reason"

If we have to be careful about the word "literal" when we move
back from the modern period to the sixteenth century, the same
is as true, if not more so, in the case of the word "reason" and its
cognates, including "rationalism." These words have, of course, a
complicated history in their own right which we cannot examine
here. But the controversies on these points which resurfaced in
the sixteenth century have continued to rumble on, and they
affect the way in which people discuss authority in our own day.

Tertullian famously asked, at the end of the second century,
"What has Athens to do with Jerusalem?"—in other words, what
has unaided philosophical reason to do with the revelation of God
in Jesus Christ? He himself, however, was no slouch when it came
to philosophically acute rhetoric; and this leaves open the question
of how, and at what level, human reason and clarity of thought
and discourse make their contributions to Christian understanding. Thomas Aquinas established the great synthesis which held
together the theology of the high Middle Ages. Scholars continue
to debate the extent to which he believed that there were some
things, including the existence of God, which one could know

with unaided human "reason"—that is, without the benefit of the special revelation given in scripture and tradition themselves, which of course remained enormously important for Thomas.

This question, of how much one could know without special revelation, burst into flame again in the early Reformation, with Luther angrily confronting Erasmus over the question of whether human will and understanding are capable of grasping the gospel, or whether original sin has so darkened the mind as to leave it, despite some elements of insight, enslaved, unable to help itself, and always in need of grace and revelation. (The parallel between the Reformation doctrine of justification by faith apart from works and knowing God by special revelation rather than native human capacity continues to be important at various levels.) The question was never satisfactorily resolved in the first generation of the Reformation, perhaps not least since the Reformers were themselves appealing to the "plain sense of scripture" over against the complexities of medieval exegesis, and the question of what counts as the "plain sense" is itself, of course, a matter of reasoned judgment.

This adds a further complexity to the question of the "senses" of scripture, since the "plain sense," a concept advanced, paradoxically, for the sake of polemic rather than clarity, is not the same thing as the "literal sense" as explored above. The "literal sense" might indeed be anything but plain, if the passage was itself complex and convoluted. The word "plain" inevitably introduces a subjective element, inviting the riposte, "Plain to whom?" which anticipates some of the problems we shall presently meet in relation to "reason" within the modern world.

In England, in particular, matters came to a head in the controversies of the second half of the sixteenth century. The Puritan movement, hoping at last to bring some kind of Calvinism to England as it had to Scotland, argued that since scripture alone was authoritative, only those customs and ceremonies should be admitted into the life of the church which were explicitly authorized by scripture itself. Against them, Richard Hooker (ca. 1554–1600) expounded a theory which, while firmly reemphasizing the basic Reformation doctrines such as justification by faith, looked back in other ways to Aquinas and the holistic medieval worldview. He insisted that all reality is governed by natural law, which is itself supremely rational, deriving from, and being the expression of, God's own supreme "reason." He saw the Puritans as following an impossibly simplistic agenda. Human society develops and changes, he pointed out, and the church, itself at one level a human society, has an organic rather than a static life, and must grow and change appropriately. As it does so, it will inevitably go beyond what scripture explicitly teaches, as, for example, the great creeds themselves undeniably do. The methods of church govern-ment, one of the particular points at issue at the time, will inevita-bly change and develop as well. Hooker's insistence on "reason" was therefore not at all a way of undervaluing scripture, but rather of ensuring that the community which based itself on scripture could have an appropriate healthy life and growth, not blundering forward as it were in the dark, but moving ahead by the light of reason, itself informed by scripture and in harmony with the natural law which stemmed from the creator God in the first place. Scripture remained central, but this God-given and scripture-informed reason enabled the church to develop in ways consistent with, though not necessar-ily envisaged by, scripture's explicit statements.

This is the point at which we can see to good advantage what Hooker meant by "reason," as distinct from the way the word has often been used subsequently. One of the many ironies of the Ref-ormation is that it was the Puritan emphasis on the right of indi-vidual interpretation of scripture which paved the way (once the element of godly devotion was removed, along with heavy-handed ecclesial authorities) for that rationalism which, from the eighteenth century onward, insisted that one could be the master of one's fate, the captain of one's own soul—guided by human reason alone, and thus able to cut loose from the teachings both of scripture and of the church. Hooker would have been horrified. For him, "reason" was part of a total natural order which led the mind up to the one true God, who had been fully and finally revealed in Jesus Christ. The thought of "reason" as an entirely separate source of information, which could then be *played off against* scripture and/or tradition, flies in the face of his whole way of thinking. Part of the legacy of Hooker, making some of the riches of medieval thought reaccessible within a Reformation framework, was precisely that holistic worldview which insists, not that scripture should be judged at the bar of "reason" and found wanting, but that in reading and interpreting scripture we must do so not arbitrarily, but with clear thinking and informed historical judgment.

This, of course, now seems to us to beg the same question as was done by the Reformers' notion of "plain sense": Whose clear thinking, and whose informed historical judgment, will count? But this projects us forward into the period when that question was put on hold, and when an apparently neutral "reason" became the arbiter against which scripture itself would be judged and found wanting.

6.

The Challenge of the Enlightenment

We are all children, grandchildren, or at least stepchildren of the eighteenth-century Enlightenment, and have cause to be both grateful for the consequent privileges and anxious about some of the consequent problems. (Even those parts of the world not originally affected by the Enlightenment, which was basically a phenomenon of western Europe and North America, have now been well and truly brought within its scope through the energetic globalization of trade, finance, television and tourism.) As it has become fashionable to question the assumptions and activities of the Enlightenment, it is worth saying from the start that it brought many blessings to the world. Science and technology have worked wonders (nobody wants to be treated by a premodern dentist) as well as catastrophes (gas chambers and atom bombs would have been technically impossible three hundred years ago). More particularly, its insistence on asking and researching historical questions has produced floods of light on many areas of vital importance to Christian thought, even though the negative side of this same insistence has often been a rationalistic skepticism which has chipped away at the very foundations of Christianity itself.

The Enlightenment's Attempt to Undermine Orthodox Christianity through Rationalism—a New Twist to "Reason"

The Enlightenment (whose leading thinkers include Hume, Voltaire, Thomas Jefferson, and Kant) was, in fact, for the most part an explicitly anti-Christian movement. Part of the ambiguity of living as a Christian in the "modern" (by which people normally mean the post-Enlightenment) world is the challenge to negotiate, and work out in practice, which of its assertions must be politely denied, which of its challenges may be taken up and by what means, and which of its accomplishments must be welcomed and enhanced. Although postmodernity has challenged a good deal of the Enlightenment worldview, most people today in the Western world, and many elsewhere as well, still assume several elements of that worldview as the only possible way of looking at the world. The negotiation and working out required is therefore inevitably complex.

In particular, the Enlightenment insisted on "reason" as the central capacity of human beings, enabling us to think and act correctly; it therefore regarded human beings as by nature rational and good. Reason was to be the arbiter of which religious and theological claims could be sustained (note Kant's famous work *Religion within the Limits of Reason Alone*). This meant that many Enlightenment thinkers tended toward atheism. Those who retained some belief in a divine being tended toward an abstract, non-trinitarian theism, or simply deism (acknowledging a distant, remote God), rather than mainline Christian belief. This context has had a profound effect, at several levels, on the way people read the Bible and think about its authority. Much of what has been written about the Bible in the last two hundred years has either been following through the Enlightenment's program, or reacting to it, or negotiating some kind of halfway house in between.

Reading the Bible within the World of the Enlightenment

In particular, the rise of historical biblical scholarship appears to be at least two-edged. First, the Enlightenment issued a necessary and salutary challenge to the church, not altogether unlike that issued by the Reformers two centuries earlier: scripture must be read historically, looking for original meanings, without assuming that it would simply state, in perhaps simpler form, what the much later church had said. This program continues to this day: it is only recently that it has been widely acknowledged, for instance, that the phrase "son of God" in many New Testament writings does not automatically mean "the second person of the Trinity," but is a title which, to a first-century Jew, would have carried messianic rather than "divine" overtones (so that the high Christology which the New Testament undoubtedly asserts is to be understood within that framework).

Second, however, from the eighteenth century onward, several historians working from within the Enlightenment project made deliberate attempts to demonstrate that such readings would in fact undermine central Christian claims. They would prove, it was asserted, that the Bible could be faulted on matters of history (it says certain things happened, but they did not), on matters of science (it said God created the world in seven days, but we now know it happened through a long period of evolution), and on matters of morality (it displays God telling the Israelites to slaughter the Canaanites and Amalekites, for example). These are all part of the standard attack mounted against Christianity from within modernism as a whole.

This, too, continues to the present day—every time, for instance, another book appears in which someone "writing as a historian" has examined the origins of Christian faith from a "neutral" perspective and found them wanting. Publishers, like journalists, still like to play tunes on the old Enlightenment organ, even though serious thinkers for these past few decades have long since realized that there is no such thing as a neutral perspective on anything. Much biblical scholarship, then, has for two centuries been poised between the necessary and exciting task of historical investigation and the polemical use of rationalistic historiography as a deliberate weapon against the claims of the church. Some, admittedly, have cut loose and declared that the whole Enlightenment project was so flawed that we should give up historical exegesis and rely on what the church has always said scripture meant. I think I know what the Reformers, not least John Calvin, would have said to that.

Since both of these two aims—historical investigation and rationalistic historiography used as a weapon against the church—claimed some continuity with those of the Protestant Reformers, the Protestant heartlands of biblical scholarship have often found it hard to distinguish between the necessity of historical scholarship (if any reading of the text is to stand up in its original sense, let alone claim any kind of "authority") and the very different appeal, implicit in much Enlightenment reading, to "reason" not as an insistence that exegesis must make sense within an overall view of God and the wider world (as in Hooker), but as a separate "source" in its own right. This has resulted in what we now understand as "rationalism," with its manifold reductive and skeptical readings which scorned the previously held central beliefs of Christians as "out of date," "premodern," etc.—a scorn still often expressed in both popular and scholarly circles, despite the attacks that have increasingly been mounted against the whole Enlightenment project, as we shall see. And in the face of such scorn, often all that is left of "the authority of scripture" is the notion that scripture gives us access to a particular type of religious experience which we might be encouraged to emulate. This is not only a very thin and unsatisfying substitute for the real, full-blooded thing, but is also actually inherently unstable, since of course the New Testament bears witness (not that this was its main purpose) to all kinds of "religious experiences," including several of which the writers clearly disapprove. The nemesis of this kind of approach is met when scholars suggest, as they have often done of late, that this legitimates all those early experiences which the writers of the New Testament themselves try to rule out. At that point, the phrase "authority of scripture" has been deconstructed to the vanishing point.

The Enlightenment's Alternative View of History's Climax

Behind their overt historical skepticism, the deeper motives of Enlightenment thinkers had to do with the effort to persuade their contemporaries that humankind had now at last come of age. All history, declared Voltaire, had been a progressive struggle toward this new, reason-based culture. Indeed, the idea of *progress* is one of the Enlightenment's most enduring legacies. When people say, as they often do, "In this day and age . . ." or "Now that we're living in the twenty-first century . . ." they are invoking the implicit notion that ever since the eighteenth century the world has been reordering itself by an inexorable movement of moral, social, and cultural rationalization in which old rules and beliefs have been either left behind or, if retained, tamed and brought into line with reason itself. The world has entered a new era, declared the philosophers, and now everything is different.

This meant that the Enlightenment was offering its own rival *eschatology,* a secular analogue to the biblical picture of God's Kingdom inaugurated by Jesus. Christianity had declared that God's Kingdom had been decisively inaugurated by Jesus himself, particularly through his death and resurrection. This sense of a one-off historical moment in the first century, however, had been so muted in much Christian theology—eschatology being replaced by systems of salvation and ethics—that the Enlightenment's cuckoo-in-the-nest move was made all the easier, and has in fact often gone unremarked. It was this eschatological takeover bid which caused Enlightenment thinkers to pour scorn on the Bible's picture of the coming Kingdom, in a move which is still taken for granted in many circles today: first, to misrepresent it ("All the early Christians expected the world to end at once") and then to rubbish it ("They were wild fanatics, and they were proved wrong"). This "we-know-better-now" move, so characteristic of various strands within Enlightenment thought (and now forming part of the mental and emotional landscape of most modern Westerners), disguised the fact that the Enlightenment's alternative was equally wild and fanatical: the belief that world history, up until now a matter of darkness and superstition, had turned the decisive corner—in western Europe and North America in the eighteenth century!—and come out into the light, not least through science and technology.

The Enlightenment's New View of Evil

The Enlightenment thus offered to the world *a new analysis of, and solution to, the problem of evil,* standing in radical tension to those offered in classical Judaism and Christianity. The real problem of evil, it proposed, is that people are not thinking and acting rationally, and Enlightenment rationalism is going to teach them how and create the social and political conditions to make it happen. The biblical scholarship which grew up within the Enlightenment world went along for the ride, reducing the act of God in Jesus Christ to mere moral teaching and example. (It is astonishing how often today people declare that "Jesus was really just a great moral teacher" as if this were a new insight rather than a 200-year-old proposal which was blatantly reductive at the time and has never been substantiated since.) The point was this: if Enlightenment progress is solving the problem of evil, all Jesus needs to have done is to point the way, to show people what love and compassion look like. Being reasonable, people will follow his example. If they do not, they need more teaching in reason.

Much would-be Christian thought (including much would-be "biblical" Christian thought) in the last two hundred years has tacitly conceded these huge claims, turning "Kingdom of God" into "the hope for heaven after death" and treating Jesus's death, at the most, as the mechanism whereby individual sinners can receive forgiveness and hope for an otherworldly future—leaving the politicians and economists of the Enlightenment to take over the running, and as it turns out the ruining, of the world. (This political agenda, by the way, was of course a vital part of the Enlightenment project: kick "God" upstairs, make religion a matter of private piety, and then you can organize the world to your own advantage. That has been the leitmotif of the Western world ever since, the new philosophy which has so far sustained several great empires, launched huge and horribly flawed totalitarian projects, and left the contemporary world thoroughly confused. But all this must wait for another day.) Scripture itself, meanwhile, is muzzled equally by both sides. It is squelched into silence by the "secularists" who dismiss it as irrelevant, historically inaccurate, and so on—as you would expect, since it might otherwise challenge their imperial dreams. Equally worrying, if not more so, it is squashed out of shape by many of the devout, who ignore its global, cosmic, and justice-laden message and treat it only as the instrument of personal piety and the source of true doctrine about eternal salvation. Secular and sacred readings—and the scholarship that has jostled between the two—have connived to produce the shallow readings which, as we saw in the prologue, constitute our immediate problem.

The Muddled Debates of Modern Biblical Scholarship

The biblical scholarship of the last two hundred years has thus never been "neutral" or "objective," despite repeated claims. Rather, it enjoys—or, as it may be, suffers—a complex dialogical relation with its contemporary cultures. In particular, it has been interwoven with the various political influences at work in Europe during the period, especially the Nazi movement (one thinks of great scholars like Gerhard Kittel, who edited the world-famous *Theological Dictionary of the New Testament,* and who was deeply involved in the anti-Semitic mood of the time) and the reaction to it in favor of a "Jewish" understanding of early Christianity, exemplified in the work of scholars like W. D. Davies. Ironically, the claim to "objectivity" among historical scholars has meant that this kind of contextualizing of their work has not often been highlighted. The one thing it is no longer possible to do is to claim that "modern biblical studies" have come to the kind of fixed and unalterable conclusions that used to be taught in colleges and seminaries—an important point, since many who now debate major issues in the life of the church were educated in that way, and their reading and use of scripture has been, to say the least, significantly skewed as a result.

In fact, as many new waves of scholarship have shown, all it takes is for someone to come at the evidence from a new angle (say, in a new book on Jesus such as E. P. Sanders's *Jesus and Judaism* [SCM, 1985]), and all sorts of things previously thought to be unhistorical—in this case, Jesus's understanding of his own vocation in terms of the restoration of Israel—suddenly take center stage and become not only historically comprehensible but compelling. This is not to say that history can make no firm advances; indeed, I regard the work of Sanders and others like him as offering major and important ways forward, though still needing development and correction, as I and many others have tried to show. Most of today's biblical scholars are aware that they and their debating partners write from within contexts with which they and their scholarship are in constant interaction, and that their work must be judged accordingly.

What does it mean, within this setting, to appeal to "the authority of scripture"? This phrase is sometimes used as a way of saying, "A plague on all your scholarship; we just believe the Bible." This is simply unsustainable. Without scholars to provide Greek lexicons and translations based on them, few today could read the New Testament. Without scholarship to explain the world of the first century, few today could begin to understand it (as often becomes painfully evident when people without such explanations try to read it aloud, let alone expound it). Scholarship of some sort is always assumed; what the protest often means, unfortunately, is that the speakers prefer the scholarship implicit in their early training, which is now simply taken for granted as common knowledge, to the bother of having to wake up mentally and think fresh thoughts. Again and again, such older scholarship, and such older traditions of reading, turn out to be flawed or in need of supplementing. Today's and tomorrow's will be just the same, of course, but this does not absolve us from constantly trying to do better, from the never-ending attempt to understand scripture more fully. It is my own experience that such attempts regularly result in real advances (measured not least in terms of the deep and many-sided sense that is made of the text), and that even making the effort almost always results in fresh pastoral and homiletic insights. To affirm "the authority of scripture" is precisely *not* to say, "We know what scripture means and don't need to raise any more questions." It is always a way of saying that the church in each generation must make fresh and rejuvenated efforts to understand scripture more fully and live by it more thoroughly, even if that means cutting across cherished traditions.

This applies not least when the traditions in question refer to themselves as "biblical." There are always some who are ready, on hearing a new interpretation, to search the scriptures afresh to see if these things are so (Acts 17:11). But there are always others whose reaction to any new proposal is to insist that since great preachers and teachers of old have said what a particular passage means, there can be nothing to add—and that even the attempt to say something new is somehow impious or arrogant. Again, there is no doubt what Martin Luther would have said to an argument like that.

In fact, those who refuse the attempt to think freshly about the Bible are often shutting themselves up inside one particular kind of post-Enlightenment Western worldview—the "fundamentalist" one, in which all kinds of things in the gospels and Paul have been screened out, despite the claim to be "biblical." Such screened-out features include the inescapably political dimension of the New Testament, and (not unconnected with this) the messiahship of Jesus (fundamentalism normally jumps from the word "Christ," not to first-century meanings of "Messiah," but to the divinity of Jesus, which the New Testament establishes on quite other grounds). The protest of that kind of fundamentalism against the "liberalism" of so-called modernist biblical scholarship (which often held the form of religion but denied its power) is simply a battle between one kind of Enlightenment vision and another. When we look at that sad polarization, the only bright side is the wry amusement of noting the extreme closed-mindedness of those who, having learned a "liberal" position thirty or forty years ago, now assume that by repeating it like a mantra they are still as "liberal" and "modern" now as they were then.

"Literal" and "Non-Literal"

This standoff sometimes expresses itself in terms of the polarization between "literalist" and "non-literalist" interpretations. As we have seen, this use of "literal" and similar terms is significantly different from the use of such words in the sixteenth-century controversies, and those who call themselves "literalists" in this modern sense should not thereby imagine that they are invoking the support of the Reformers. In fact, the labels have come to designate not just different hermeneutical proposals but, especially in the United States, entire worldviews. This makes serious discussion of disputed texts almost impossible, as implied charges of "guilt by association" echo to and fro ("You're really just a literalistic fundamentalist," or "You're really just an unbelieving liberal").

This false either/or polarization results in serious misperceptions. Not all who try to follow the Bible in detail as well as outline are fundamentalists; nor are they all guilty of those cultural, intellectual, and moral failings which North American (and other) liberals perceive in North American (and other) conservatives. Equally, not all who question some elements of New Testament teaching, or its applicability to the present day, are "liberals" in the sense pejoratively intended by North American conservatives or traditionalists. The extraordinary and sometimes horrible excesses of behavior on both sides in the localized social and cultural politics of North America must of course be borne in mind during debate. So, too, must the oddity (as it seems to an outside observer) that those who are most keen on "conservative" Christianity on some issues often choose to ignore what the Bible says about loving one's enemies and about economic justice, and choose to forget that many of the earliest and finest exponents of Christian scripture—the early church fathers—were firmly opposed to the death penalty. If we want to be literal-minded, let us take the relevant texts on such subjects seriously. But the contemporary cultural, social, and political resonances cannot be allowed to determine the meaning or relevance of texts and themes. Abuse of scripture has been going on from the very first, as 2 Peter 3:16 indicates, and it does not mean either that scripture is now useless or that its proper use is beyond recapture. (On all this, see further chapter 5.)

Historical Exegesis: Still Basic, but No Guarantee of Modernism's "Assured Results"

The problem of how to use "modernist" biblical scholarship within the church has thus been exacerbated by the local culture-wars of North America—which happens now to be the major center of biblical scholarship, having supplanted Germany in this respect over the last generation or so. But this problem ought to look very different (though this has not yet been widely noticed) in the light of the detailed and careful work of the last half-century in highlighting and exploring the historical and cultural context, Jewish and Greco-Roman alike, of early Christianity. Many of the old "consensus" positions (e.g., that Paul could not have written Ephesians and Colossians; that forms of gospel tradition which exhibited "Jewish" characteristics must be later developments than those which matched Hellenistic ones) grew straight out of the Enlightenment's rationalistic Protestantism, which screened out, among other things, both the Jewishness of the New Testament and anything that smacked of "early Catholicism." We have come to a point in scholarship, quite apart from considerations of applicability to the church, where we need to take a fresh look at all elements of the picture. An obvious example is historical-Jesus research, whose climate has changed drastically over the last thirty years.

The fact that I have criticized the "literal/non-literal" polarization does not mean that I am indifferent to the question of whether the events written about in the gospels actually took place. Far from it. It is just that it will not do to repeat irrelevant slogans and imagine that one has thereby settled the matter. There is a great gulf fixed between those who want to prove the historicity of everything reported in the Bible in order to demonstrate that the Bible is "true" after all and those who, committed to living under the authority of scripture, remain open to what scripture itself actually teaches and emphasizes. Which is the bottom line: "proving the Bible to be true" (often with the effect of saying, "So we can go on thinking what we've always thought"), or taking it so seriously that we allow it to tell us things we'd never heard before and didn't particularly want to hear?

To suggest that we should take a fresh look at the problems is precisely *not* to advocate a return to premodern readings, as those who want to perpetuate Enlightenment modernism will of course suggest. On the contrary: it is to go further into serious historical work than modernism (for its own reasons) was prepared to do. When we do this, we discover again and again that many of the problems or "contradictions" discovered by modernist critical study were the result of projecting alien worldviews onto the text. We have far better lexicons today than modernism did; new editions of more and more ancient texts; more archaeological and numismatic discoveries than most of us can cope with. We should gratefully use all these historical resources. When we do so, as I have argued elsewhere, we will discover that quite a bit of the old "modernist" consensus is challenged on the grounds to which it originally appealed—namely, serious historical reconstruction. As one recent writer points out, "Its critics have little choice but to pay the Enlightenment the compliment of turning its own weapons against it" (M. J. Inwood, in *The Oxford Companion to Philosophy*, ed. T. Honderich [OUP, 1995], 237).

The Enlightenment appeals to history; but this should hold no terrors for the Christian. If it is true that the living God lived, died, and rose again in first-century Palestine, such events offer themselves for scrutiny, much as, according to the story, the risen Jesus did when facing the skeptic Thomas (John 20:24–29). It might be better to believe without seeing, as Jesus said to Thomas on that occasion; but for those who have asked the skeptic's question, Christianity should be ready to give an answer about what really happened within history and how, within the historian's own proper discipline, we can know that with the kind of "knowledge" appropriate to, and available within, historical research. Indeed, I would go further. In addressing the question, we might discover things about what scripture is saying which our own traditions had conveniently screened out. Perhaps it is only under pressure from our cultured despisers that we will get down to the task we should never have abandoned, that of continually trying to understand and live by our foundation texts even better than our predecessors. Again, that is precisely what living by the authority of scripture looks like in practice.

Postmodernity's Appropriate Challenge to Modernity: Necessary Corrective and Nihilistic Deconstruction

Modernism and its readings have, as I have already suggested, been simultaneously under a different kind of attack, from the post-modern movement. Postmodernism, by unmasking the power interests latent in texts and movements, not least those of the last two hundred years, has offered a sustained ideological challenge not only to many ancient and modern texts but to modernism itself—particularly the economic and cultural hegemony of the Western world which rests on the achievements of the Enlighten-ment. We have seen all kinds of fresh readings of biblical texts— feminist, post-Holocaust, ethnic, post-colonial, and so forth—all of which have discovered passages which have been used, and which some have suggested were intended to be used, as "texts of terror," that is, weapons of oppression or worse.

An obvious example is the cry of "His blood be on us and on our children" in Matthew 27:25, which became a storm center in the making, and discussion, of Mel Gibson's film *The Passion of the Christ*. Another well-known example of a deconstructionist read-ing is the analysis of Mark's portrayal of Herod Antipas (6:17–29), in which the story is shown to reflect a typically "male" perspec-tive, with Herod only marginally guilty of the death of John the

Baptist, being the helpless victim of his seductive stepdaughter and his scheming wife. Sometimes texts acquire new and unwelcome meanings because of fresh political events. It is shocking but perhaps inevitable that Palestinian Christians find it difficult or impossible to sing those Psalms which speak of Israel winning military victories over its enemies.

Such deconstructive readings, many will conclude, have done us a service by pointing out the ways in which texts *can* be heard, whether or not they were intended that way. They have also had the effect (in this respect simply increasing the force of modernist rationalism) of removing texts from the implicit canon, while sometimes offering alternative candidates for inclusion. In some cases they render whole books unusable because those writings are deemed guilty of what the postmodern Western world regards, in its new and highly self-righteous judgmentalism, as unforgivable ideological sins. Deconstruction of standard ways of reading texts is by no means always a negative or destructive thing to do; it may have the effect of jolting us out of comfortable half-truths to see something which is really there in the text and to which we had not previously paid attention. But often deconstruction has been used, quite explicitly, to place a warning sign ("Danger! Ideological prejudices!") against the text as a whole.

Postmodernity's effect on contemporary Western readings of scripture is thus, as with much else in the movement, essentially negative. Postmodernity agrees with modernity in scorning both the eschatological claim of Christianity and its solution to the problem of evil, but without putting any alternative in place. All we can do with the Bible, if postmodernity is left in charge, is to play with such texts as give us pleasure, and issue warnings against those that give pain to ourselves or to others who attract our (usually selective) sympathy. *This is where a good deal of the Western church now finds itself.* The fact that this position is merely assumed, not usually spelled out, makes it all the more potent, since postmodernity is currently what "feels right" in Western culture, and does not open itself to challenge by coming out into the open. Indeed, challenges are routinely dismissed as an attempt to go back to modernity or even premodernity, leaving us with a fine irony: an ideology which declares that all ideologies are power plays, yet which sustains its own position by ruling out all challenges a priori. Much criticism, both modern and postmodern, has thus left the church, after years of highly funded research in seminaries and colleges, less able to use the Bible in anything like the way which Jesus and the earliest Christians envisaged. This is the reason for the biblical vacuum at the heart of many of the so-called mainline churches on both sides of the North Atlantic and elsewhere. And this is why we are reduced to shouting matches about biblical authority.

But supposing there might be a better way?

Postmodernity's Impotence

We cannot evade the problem, as fundamentalism does, simply by appealing to an a priori argument ("The Bible says . . ."). However, at the level of cultural movements, we are bound to take note both of the implicit cultural imperialism within modernism (which postmodernism itself has unmasked, but also in another way perpetuated by its implicit claim that only the postmodernists really see what's been going on) and of the failure of postmodern criticism actually to do anything about it. As Nicholas Boyle has pointed out (*Who Are We Now?* [University of Notre Dame Press, 1998]), all that deconstruction achieves is a nihilism in which the only relief is a kind of hermeneutical narcissism, taking one's pleasure with the text and letting the rest of the world go by unnoticed. It cannot successfully challenge real evil, since every challenge can itself be deconstructed into the hidden motivations of the challenger(s); and scripture itself is thereby muzzled into silent connivance with radical evil.

Thus to point out a "masculine" bias in Mark's telling of one story, and so to cast moral aspersions on the whole of Mark's project, could result in our failing to see that Mark's story of God's Kingdom breaking in through Jesus's death and resurrection constitutes a very profound political and theological critique of the ruling pagan empire whose soldiers killed the Jewish Messiah (see, for instance, Mark 10:42–45). Another example: to suggest, as is sometimes done, that the apparent "patriarchy" of the household codes of Ephesians and Colossians renders those books unusable today means, once more, that their vision of the church as the renewed and united people of God, who by their very existence offer a powerful and unanswerable challenge to pagan religion and empire, goes unheard. (See the new book by Brian Walsh and Sylvia Keesmaat, *Colossians Remixed* [IVP, 2004].)

As I shall suggest presently, a narratival and "critical realist" reading of scripture offers a way forward through the postmodern morass and out the other side—a task that appears the more urgent as the great world empire of our own day proceeds to impose its economic, political, military, and cultural will on the world, while the proponents of radical positions in today's "culture wars" remain impotent to stop it.

What about "Experience"?

Whenever people today talk about "authority" within the church, a regular appeal is made on behalf of "experience." Indeed, though this has never been accepted within official formulations, many church leaders now speak of "scripture, tradition, reason, and experience" as though the well-known three-legged stool had now been upgraded by the addition of another leg of the same type as the other three. The main historical source for this is the interpretation by some subsequent writers of the emphasis on "experience" in the thought of John Wesley. Indeed, some have spoken of a "Wesleyan Quadrilateral," a phrase Wesley himself never used. For Wesley himself, scripture remained the primary authority; the "experience" upon which he insisted was the living experience of God's love and the power of the Holy Spirit, through which what the Bible said was proved true in the life of the believer. It is quite an illegitimate use of all this to see "experience" as a separate source of authority to be played off against scripture itself, though this move is now frequent, almost routine, in many theological circles ("Scripture says . . . tradition says . . . reason says . . . but experience says . . . and so that's what we go with"). Sometimes this question has been played back into the study of early Christianity, as though the really "normative" thing about the early church, and indeed the New Testament, were its testimony to something called "early Christian experience." This is wholly in line with both modernist and postmodernist agendas, but I regard it as misleading. Adding a fourth leg to a three-legged stool often makes it unstable.

Actually, for a start, "scripture, tradition, and reason" were never the same *kind* of thing. The image of the stool with three matching legs is itself misleading. They are not so much like apples, pears, and oranges as like apples, elephants, and screwdrivers. As we have seen, a long line of theologians from Aquinas through Hooker to many writers today would insist that "tradition" is the legacy of what the church has said when reflecting on scripture, and "reason" is the rule of discourse by which such reflection is saved from random nonsense and integrated into a holistic view of God and the world. This too, however, can only be part of the story, and might imply a more solid and fixed form for "tradition" and "reason" than the story of the church warrants.

To change the picture, scripture, tradition, and reason are not like three different bookshelves, each of which can be ransacked for answers to key questions. Rather, scripture is the bookshelf; tradition is the memory of what people in the house have read and understood (or perhaps misunderstood) from that shelf; and reason is the set of spectacles that people wear in order to make sense of what they read—though, worryingly, the spectacles have varied over time, and there are signs that some readers, using the "reason" available to them, have severely distorted the texts they were reading. "Experience" is something different again, referring to the effect on readers of what they read, and/or the worldview, the life experience, the political circumstances, and so on, within which that reading takes place.

This can be seen—in "experience"!—by the chaos that results if "experience" is allowed to be the final arbiter. Whether in official statistics or in anecdotal evidence, the "experience" of Christians, and of everyone else for that matter, always and inevitably comes up with several simultaneous and incompatible stories. "Experience" is far too slippery for the concept to stand any chance of providing a stable basis sufficient to serve as an "authority," unless what is meant is that, as the book of Judges wryly puts it, everyone should simply do that which is right in their own eyes. And that, of course, means that there is no authority at all. Indeed, the stress on "experience" has contributed materially to that form of pluralism, verging on anarchy, which we now see across the Western world.

But there is a more profound problem to be addressed, indeed a logical problem. The "experience" of Christians, and of churches, is itself *that over which and in the context of which the reading of scripture exercises its authority*. It is precisely because "experience" is fluid and puzzling, and because all human beings including devout Christians are prey to serious and multilayered self deception, including in their traditions and their reasoning (as Jeremiah lamented, the heart is deceitful above all things [17:9]), that "authority" is needed in the first place. That, too, is one of the main things we discover by "experience"! To speak of "experience" as an *authority,* then, is to admit that the word "authority" itself is being dismantled, unable now to function either as "court of appeal" in the old wooden sense or, in the more biblical sense, as "that through which God exercises Kingdom-establishing power." That dismantling—the muzzling of the challenge of God to the idolatrous world—was one of the main (anti-Christian) aims of the Enlightenment, continued in a different mode within postmodernity. If "experience" is itself a *source* of authority, we can no longer be *addressed* by a word which comes from beyond ourselves. At this point, theology and Christian living cease to be rooted in God himself, and are rooted instead in our own selves; in other words, they become a form of idolatry in which we exchange the truth about God for a human-made lie. This, or something like it, is what we find with the popular modern varieties of Gnosticism, in which the highest religious good is self-discovery and then being "true" to the self thus discovered. But to elevate that imperative (now radically challenged by postmodernity, though this is not usually noticed in the relevant discussions) to the supreme status now claimed for it is to take a large step away from all known forms of orthodox Christianity.

"Experience" and Context

The positive force of the appeal to "experience" is much better expressed in terms of the *context within which* we hear scripture. Experience, as the necessary subjective pole of all knowing, is the place where we stand as we hear God's word, know his love, and understand his wisdom. It is vital that Christians should "experience" the power and love of God in their own lives. This is never simply a mechanical application of "God's authority," as though human beings were mere ciphers rather than image-bearers. And, precisely because of the problem of evil within us as well as within the world (the problem which the Enlightenment sought to belittle), we need to be addressed and challenged within that place, that subjectivity, not simply informed that we are all right as we are.

We could put it like this. "Experience" is what grows by itself in the garden. "Authority" is what happens when the gardener wants to affirm the goodness of the genuine flowers and vegetables by uprooting the weeds in order to let beauty and fruitfulness triumph over chaos, thorns, and thistles. An over-authoritarian church, paying no attention to experience, solves the problem by paving the garden with concrete. An over-experiential church solves the (real or imagined) problem of concrete (rigid and "judgmental" forms of faith) by letting anything and everything grow unchecked, sometimes labeling concrete as "law" and so celebrating any and every weed as "grace." God's affirmation of us as created in his image, with all that this implies, always includes his challenge to us as we distort that image through idolatry, and his promise to forgive and remake us, through the new covenant established in Jesus, as part of the new creation that has already begun and will one day be completed. And of course (because of our propensity to self-deception) we constantly need to check, against scripture, whether we are allowing the word of God's grace in the gospel, and God's reaffirmation of us as made in his image, to validate what is in fact an idolatrous and distorted form of humanness. When, through letting scripture be the vehicle of God's judging and healing authority in our communities and individual lives, we really do "experience" God's affirmation, then we shall know as we are known.

7.

Misreadings of Scripture

Within this complex cultural context, it is not surprising that all kinds of misreadings of scripture have grown up, both among those who count themselves as Bible-believers and among those who distance themselves from that label while claiming some continuity at least with the biblical tradition. Many of these misreadings are now so common that they are taken for granted in large segments of the church.

At the risk of sustaining a polarization I regard as misleading, we might instance them in two blocks. What follows is a short list; many more examples could be found. I here summarize wildly for reasons of space, and at the obvious risk of caricature. Each of the categories could of course be explained and exemplified at much greater length.

Misreadings of the "Right"

To begin with, I offer the many positions regularly thought of as "right wing" which are based on, or involve, a serious misreading of scripture:

A. The openly dualistic "rapture" reading of 1 Thessalonians 4 (as in the hugely popular and blatantly right-wing American Left Behind series), which ironically lives in close symbiosis with (B) below.

B. The explicitly materialist "prosperity gospel" understanding of biblical promises.

C. The support of slavery. (Scripture always struggled to humanize an institution it could not expect to eradicate; by privileging the Exodus narrative, it constantly appealed to a controlling story of the God who set slaves free; at some points, e.g., Philemon, it set a time-bomb beside the whole system.)

D. The endemic racism of much of Western culture. (Neo-apartheid groups still try to base racial ideologies on scripture.)

E. Undifferentiated reading of the Old and New Testaments, which of course exists in symbiosis with (F) below.

F. Unacknowledged and arbitrary pick-and-mix selection of an implicit canon-within-the-canon. (Few Christians have offered animal sacrifice or rejected pork, shellfish, etc., but few know why; some churches are tough on sexual offenses but not on anger and violence, and others are the other way around; few today even notice the regular biblical prohibitions against usury.)

G. The application of "new Israel" ideas (e.g., a reading of Deuteronomy) to various Enlightenment projects. (The United States is the obvious example, but interestingly the same ideology can be found, transposed into a French Roman Catholic key, in Quebec.)

H. Support for the death penalty (opposed by many of the early church fathers).

I. Discovery of "religious" meanings and exclusion of "political" ones, thus often tacitly supporting the social status quo; this happily coexists in some cultures with (A) above.

J. Readings of Paul in general and Romans in particular which screen out the entire Jewish dimension through which alone that letter makes sense; this often exists in symbiosis with (K) below.

K. Attempted "biblical" support for the modern state of Israel as the fulfillment of scriptural prophecy.

L. An overall failure to pay attention to context and hermeneutics.

Much of this, alas, characterizes so-called "conservative" Christianity. Much "liberal" Christianity, seeing this, and rightly associating it with a subculture with which it has other quarrels as well, defines itself explicitly in opposition ("freeing the Bible from fundamentalism," and so forth).

Misreadings of the "Left"

The preceding list is balanced by the equally routine misreadings by what is thought of as the "left wing":

A. The claim to "objectivity" or to a "neutral" reading of the text (the classic modernist position).

B. The claim that modern history or science has either "disproved the Bible" or made some of its central claims redundant, undesirable, or unbelievable.

C. The "cultural relativity" argument: "The Bible is an old book from a different culture, so we can't take it seriously in the modern world."

D. Rationalist rewritings of history, which assume as a fixed starting-point what the Enlightenment wanted to prove (that, say, some aspects of the story of Jesus "couldn't have happened") but has not been able to.

E. The attempt to relativize specific and often-repeated biblical teachings by appealing to a generalized "principle" which looks suspiciously Enlightenment-generated (e.g., "tolerance" or "inclusivity"); note that, when Jesus went to lunch with Zacchaeus (Luke 19:1–10), people were shocked but Zacchaeus was changed; and that, having "included" the woman taken in adultery and shown up her self-righteous accusers (John 8:1–11), Jesus told her not to sin again.

F. Caricaturing biblical teaching on some topics in order to be able to set aside its teaching on other topics: despite repeated assertions, the New Testament *does* allow divorce in certain circumstances; it *does* envisage women as apostles and deacons, and as leading in worship; it *does* (see above) do its best to humanize, and then to challenge, slavery.

G. Discovery of "political" meanings to the exclusion of "religious" ones, often without noticing that, unless there is some power unleashed by these readings, this results merely in sloganeering which provides false comfort to the faithful through a sense of their own moral insight and superiority ("I thank thee, Lord, that I am not like those non-political pietists"), but without effecting actual change in the world.

H. The proposal that the New Testament used the Old Testament in a fairly arbitrary or unwarranted fashion; sometimes, as we saw, the conclusion is drawn that we can and should use the New Testament in the same way. Standard examples include Matthew's use of Hosea (2:15) and Paul's use of the "seed" motif (Galatians 3:16). Both, in fact, depend on a nexus between Jesus and Israel which remained opaque to many Protestant scholars in the modernist period, but which is now fairly common coin within the scholarship that has paid attention to the New Testament's use of Old Testament themes and narratives.

I. The claim that the New Testament writers did not think they were writing "scripture," so that our appeal to them as such already does them violence (see pages 51–52).

J. Pointing out that the church took a while to settle on the precise canon (and that the relevant debates included some non-theological factors, e.g., political ones), and using this as an argument for discrediting the canon and privileging other books (e.g., "Thomas") which articulate a different worldview, sometimes ironically projecting this preference back into a neo-positivistic claim for an early date for the non-canonical material (see pages 62–65).

K. A skin-deep-only appeal to "contextual readings," as though by murmuring the magic word "context" one is allowed to hold the meaning and relevance of the text at arm's length.

L. The attempt to reduce "truth" to "scientific" statements on the one hand, or to deconstruct it altogether on the other.

Much of this, alas, characterizes much so-called "liberal" reading of scripture. Mainline churches and seminaries in the West have routinely assumed, and taught, that all this is assured as the result of modern scholarship, and that any attempt to challenge it at any point represents a return to an anti-intellectual premodernity— which would put in jeopardy the status, the credibility, and quite possibly the salary of the challenger. The result has been remarkable ignorance of what scripture is and teaches; an inability to use it in serious, mature, and indeed Christian ways; and, of course, a reaction by "conservative" Christians, who, seeing this, and rightly associating it with other cultural and social factors with which they also have quarrels, define themselves explicitly in opposition.

The Polarization of Debates and the Need for Fresh, Kingdom-Oriented, Historically Rooted Exegesis

It is from this root—the culturally conditioned "Bible wars" of Western culture, not least in North America—that the polarization of current debates has emerged. It is in that context, again, that one hears it said frequently that all reading of scripture is a matter of interpretation, with the implication that one person's interpretation is as good as another's. This is of course a variation on the classic postmodern position that there are no such things as texts, only interpretations, since when I read a text it "becomes" something different from what it "becomes" when you read it (Heisenberg's uncertainty principle again).

This is demonstrably flawed. It can be shown, and many (including myself) have attempted to do so, that a "critical realist" reading can take the postmodern critique fully on board and still come back with a strong case for a genuinely historical understanding. I have spelled this out in Part II of *The New Testament and the People of God* (Fortress Press, 1992). We must hear the questions and work through them to answers, refusing either to lapse back into reassertions, as though the questions did not exist, or to capitulate before their challenge. Genuine historical scholarship is still the appropriate tool with which to work at discovering more fully what pre-

cisely the biblical authors intended to say. We really do have access
to the past; granted, we see it through our own eyes, and our eyes
are culturally conditioned to notice some things and not others.
But they really do notice things, and provided we keep open the
conversation with other people who look from other perspectives,
we have a real, and not illusory, chance of finding out more or less
what really happened. It is possible to say definitely that some readings of ancient texts are historically preferable to others. (Thus, for
example, there are serious and not merely subjective ways of decid-
ing that a book which argues that Mark's gospel is really about
recovering from alcoholism—there really is such a book—is not
getting as close to the heart of the text as one which locates the
work afresh within the Jewish and Roman power struggles of its
day, and which then attempts to understand today's world of religion and empire and address it with the same gospel.) Real history
is possible; real historians do it all the time. Real, fresh, historical
readings of the Bible, measured rigorously by the canons of real
historical work, can and do yield fresh insight.

To say this is by no means to capitulate to the ideology of the
Enlightenment, as some are eager to suggest. Just because all the
builders in a particular period used inadequate designs and materials, we should not for that reason abandon building itself and live in
tents. History—both "what happened in the past" and "our study of
what happened in the past"—is part of God's world, to be investi-
gated with the proper tools. Real history needs to be integrated with
real theology, which itself (because of the incarnation) will reinforce
the urgency and the propriety of the historians' task. Only if, by
such means, we work our way through and out the other side of
today's ideological debates can we hope to gain any clarity, let alone
resolution. And only if we do so can we have any claim to be living

in accordance with, let alone under the authority of, scripture. Fortunately, as the present analysis has tried to indicate, the polarizations
of both modernism and postmodernism can be weighed in the balance of scripture, Christian tradition and reason and found wanting.
The remedy for both kinds of misreadings—and the way to work
through the postmodern critique and out the other side—is complex and urgent. That remedy is the subject of the next chapter.

8.

How to Get Back on Track

We urgently need an *integrated* view of the dense and complex phrase "the authority of scripture." Such an integrated view needs to highlight the role of the Spirit as the powerful, transformative agent. It needs to keep as its central focus the goal of God's Kingdom, inaugurated by Jesus on earth as in heaven and one day to be completed under that same rubric. It must envisage the church as characterized, at the very heart of its life, by prayerful listening to, strenuous wrestling with, humble obedience before, and powerful proclamation of scripture, particularly in the ministries of its authorized leaders. The following sections constitute suggestions on this theme.

God, Scripture, and the Church's Mission

The whole of my argument so far leads to the following major conclusion: that the shorthand phrase "the authority of scripture," when unpacked, offers a picture of God's sovereign and saving plan for the entire cosmos, dramatically inaugurated by Jesus himself, and now to be implemented through the Spirit-led life of the church *precisely as the scripture-reading community*. "Reading" in that last phrase is itself a shorthand for a whole complex of tasks to which we shall return. But the emphasis I want to insist on is that we discover what the shape and the inner life of the church ought to be only when we look first at the church's mission, and that we discover what the church's mission is only when we look first at God's purpose for the entire world, as indicated in, for instance, Genesis 1—2, Genesis 12, Isaiah 40—55, Romans 8, 1 Corinthians 15, Ephesians 1 and Revelation 21—22. We read scripture in order to be refreshed in our memory and understanding of the story within which we ourselves are actors, to be reminded where it has come from and where it is going to, and hence what our own part within it ought to be.

This means that "the authority of scripture" is most truly put into operation as the church goes to work in the world on behalf of the gospel, the good news that in Jesus Christ the living God has defeated the powers of evil and begun the work of new creation. It is with the Bible in its hand, its head, and its heart—not merely with the newspaper and the latest political fashion or scheme—that the church can go to work in the world, confident that Jesus is Lord and Caesar is not. The wisdom commended in scripture itself (e.g., Colossians 4:5–6; 1 Peter 3:15) suggests that we will not go about this work simply by telling people what the Bible says. In the power and wisdom of the Spirit, we must so understand the priorities of the gospel and the way in which they work to pull down strongholds (2 Corinthians 10:3–6) that we can articulate for ourselves, addressing particular contexts and settings, the challenge of the God who loves the world so much that he longs to rescue it from folly, oppression, and wickedness. Scripture's authority is thus seen to best advantage in its formation of the mind of the church, and its stiffening of our resolve, as we work to implement the resurrection of Jesus, and so to anticipate the day when God will make all things new, and justice, joy and peace will triumph (Ephesians 1:3–23).

Within this, scripture has a more particular role in relation to the gospel's challenge to individual human beings. The gospel by which individuals come to personal faith, and so to that radical transformation of life spoken of so often in the New Testament, is the personalizing of the larger challenge just mentioned: the call to every child, woman, and man to submit in faith to the lordship of the crucified and risen Jesus and so to become, through baptism and membership in the body of Christ, a living, breathing anticipation of the final new creation itself (see Galatians 6:15; 2 Corinthians 5:17). The power of God which acts through the gospel message to accomplish this end is regularly unleashed, as we saw, through the combination of the power of the Spirit and the spoken or written word; and, throughout the history of the Christian mission, that word is normally the word of scripture, read, preached, explained and applied. "The authority of scripture" refers not least to God's work *through* scripture to reveal Jesus, to speak in life-changing power to the hearts and minds of individuals, and to transform them by the Spirit's healing love. Though this can happen in the supposed "desert island" situation, where an individual reads the Bible all alone, it normally comes about through the work of God's people, from those who translated and published the Bible itself (even on a desert island, one is dependent on others!) to those who, like Philip with the Ethiopian eunuch in Acts 8, helped others to understand it and apply it to their own lives.

"The authority of scripture" thus makes the sense it does within the work of God's Kingdom, at every level from the cosmic and political through to the personal. Only when that all-inclusive authority is put in first place might we discover what the phrase could mean in terms of the ordering of the church's own life to enable it to be the agent of God's mission, and in terms of its challenge to every Christian to live under the authority of God in all departments of life.

In order to explore how this works, we must approach it by looking first at the continuing place of tradition and reason.

The Place of *Tradition:* Living in Dialogue with Previous Readings

Granted the role of scripture, as sketched in the previous section, within the church's God-given mission in the world, how does the church order its own life? I shall come presently to the actual mechanics of how scripture's authority (that is, God's authority exercised through scripture) works out in practice. First, though, some reflections on the role of tradition.

Paying attention to tradition means listening carefully (humbly but not uncritically) to how the church has read and lived scripture in the past. We must be constantly aware of our responsibility in the Communion of Saints, without giving our honored predecessors the final say or making them an "alternative source," independent of scripture itself. When they speak with one voice, we should listen very carefully. They may be wrong. They sometimes are. But we ignore them at our peril. The study of church history is not, ultimately, a different "subject" from the careful Christian reading of scripture. Every period, every key figure in the history of the church has left his, her, or its mark on subsequent readings of scripture, and if we are unaware of this we are to that extent less able to understand why we "naturally" read the text in this or that way.

This process of living with tradition, and of reading the Bible in its light, begins within very early Christianity itself. "Christ died for our sins according to the scriptures"; as soon as someone had said that (and, according to Luke 24, Jesus himself said something very like it), those who heard and pondered the claim were bound thereafter to read the scriptures in the light of the new proclamation. Paul spoke from time to time of the very early traditions which he took care to pass on (1 Corinthians 11:23; 1 Thessalonians 4:1). In subsequent generations, those who formulated the Apostles' Creed, and still more the great fourth-century Nicene Creed and its development in Constantinople, were providing a grid, a pattern, a model for how to read the Bible. It is not a complete and not an entirely adequate model; it makes no mention of what is central in the gospels themselves—namely, Jesus's announcement and inauguration of God's Kingdom (unless we count the clause "his Kingdom shall have no end"). But the church has always recognized it as a rich and many-sided summary of what Christians have come to believe as they have struggled with scripture and with that grateful obedience to God which constitutes characteristic Christian living.

Looking at our much more recent past, it is important for Christians today to be aware of the tradition(s) within which they themselves stand. Each tradition has much about it for which its adherents can be thankful. None is complete in itself—including those, as I have said already, that pride themselves on being "biblical." A way of assessing how valuable, and how incomplete, any tradition may be is to discern the extent to which each tradition can find itself at home in both public reading and private study of the scriptures, without resort to selective readings and exegetical trickery. That is precisely where the proper task of historical exegesis (as opposed to the improper one of trying to undermine Christian faith altogether) needs to make itself felt again and again. The challenge of living with tradition is not so much, as in official

Roman Catholic understandings, that one should let tradition and scripture flow together straightforwardly into a single stream, but that tradition should be allowed to be itself; that is, the living voice of the very human church as it struggles with scripture, sometimes misunderstanding it and sometimes gloriously getting it right. That is why the challenge comes fresh to each generation. Traditions tell us where we have come from. Scripture itself is a better guide as to where we should now be going.

The Place of *Reason:* Being Attentive to Context, to Sense, and to Wider Knowledge of All Sorts

Likewise, *reason* will mean giving up merely arbitrary or whimsical readings of texts, and paying attention to lexical, contextual, and historical considerations. Reason provides a check on unrestrained imaginative readings of texts (e.g., the proposal that Jesus was really an Egyptian freemason—a proposal solemnly advanced by a recent work of pseudo-scholarship). It will include the need to make sense. Of course, the question of what counts as "making sense," and the question of "whose rationality?" will remain contested, but not so as to render all discussion futile. It will mean giving attention to our own contexts, and the biases thereby introduced. This is why public discussions and debates, rather than shouting-matches, are such an urgent requirement. Far too much discourse on contentious issues has consisted of rhetorical moves designed to wipe one's opponent's pieces off the board before the game has begun.

"Reason" will mean giving attention to, and celebrating, the many and massive discoveries in biology, archaeology, physics, astronomy, and so on, which shed great light on God's world and the human condition. This does not, of course, mean giving in to the pressure which comes from atheistic or rationalistic science. We must never forget that science, by definition, studies the repeatable, whereas history, by definition, studies the unrepeatable. Nor can "reason" be casually conflated with "the results of modern science," as though there were a straightforward route, a kind of natural theology, from what we find in the test tube to what we can and must say about God and his Kingdom. "Reason" is more like the laws of harmony and counterpoint: it does not write tunes itself, but it forms the language within which tunes make powerful sense.

In all this, "reason" will not constitute an alternative, or independent, source to scripture and tradition. It is the necessary adjunct, the vital tool, for making sure that we are truly listening to scripture and tradition rather than to the echoes of our own voices. It is also an essential way of making sure we are listening to one another, remembering that we live together in the one world made and sustained by the one God we know in Jesus Christ. Reasoned discourse is part of God's alternative way of living, over against that of violence and chaos. That, perhaps, is part at least of the reason why Paul speaks of our being transformed by the renewal of our minds (Romans 12:2), over against being conformed to the present age, in terms of "our reasonable worship." All this is as necessary in discussing scripture as anywhere else.

Developing a Multilayered View: The Five-Act Model

We need, more especially, a *multilayered* view of scripture, corresponding to that which we discerned among the earliest Christians (see pages 53–57). We must recognize the vital importance of genre, setting, literary style, and so on, and the all-important differences these things make to how we read the relevant texts. Still more important, we must understand the crucial distinction between the Old and the New Testaments, why this distinction is there, and what it means and does not mean. If these various issues are ignored, we run once more into the sterile debate between people who say, "The Bible says . . ." and those who answer, "Yes, and the Bible also says you should stone adulterers, and you shouldn't wear clothes made of two types of cloth." We urgently need to get past this unnecessary roadblock and on to more serious engagement.

This is where my proposal about a "five-act" hermeneutic comes in (*The New Testament and the People of God,* chapter 5). As I have argued there in detail, the Bible itself offers a model for its own reading, which involves knowing where we are within the overall drama and what is appropriate within each act. The acts are: creation, "fall," Israel, Jesus, and the church; they constitute the differentiated stages in the divine drama which scripture itself offers.

Three initial explanatory notes on this model:

1. Others have developed the model differently. Since it *is* only a model I welcome the possibility of such modifications, but for our present purposes I am staying with the original one.

2. I gladly acknowledge that the final scene of the New Testament's vision of the future, as glimpsed at the end of Revelation, looks suspiciously like the start of a new play altogether, designed to begin where the present one leaves off.

3. I also freely acknowledge that this model highlights the "fall" more than many biblical writers do themselves, but without taking time to argue the point here I would stress that the story of Genesis 3 lies implicitly behind a good deal of the New Testament, by no means only Paul. Though

Jews of the first century held several quite different views about the origins of evil, the overall picture, of a good creation spoiled, is widespread and was arguably assumed more or less across the board in early Christianity.

Whether or not one adopts this particular scheme of interpretation, it is vital that we understand scripture, and our relation to it, in terms of some kind of overarching narrative which makes sense of the texts. We cannot reduce scripture to a set of "timeless truths" on the one hand, or to mere fuel for devotion on the other, without being deeply disloyal, at a structural level, to scripture itself.

Within the scheme I am proposing, we are currently living in the fifth act, the time of the church. This act began with Easter and Pentecost; its opening scenes were the apostolic period itself; its charter text is the New Testament; its goal, its intended final scene, is sketched clearly in such passages as Romans 8, 1 Corinthians 15 and Revelation 21–22. The key point of the whole model, which forms the heart of the multilayered view of how "the authority of scripture" actually works, runs as follows: Those who live in this fifth act have an ambiguous relationship with the four previous acts, not because they are being disloyal to them but precisely because they are being loyal to them as part of the story. If someone in the fifth act of *All's Well That Ends Well* were to start repeating speeches from earlier acts, instead of those which belonged to the fifth act itself, the whole play would begin to unravel. We must act in the appropriate manner for *this* moment in the story; this will be in direct continuity with the previous acts (we are not free to jump suddenly to another narrative, a different play altogether), but such continuity also implies discontinuity, a moment where genuinely new things can and do happen. We must be ferociously loyal to what has gone before and cheerfully open about what must come next.

Thus, for instance:

1. We cannot assume we are living in a Garden of Eden situation, a world without evil; so we cannot argue directly from "the way things are" to "the way things should be." We can in principle argue from the way things *were* (i.e., in Genesis 1 and 2) to the way things should be. This, however, is difficult in practice, both because Genesis 1 and 2 are brief and stylized, and because the redemption, when it arrives, is promised not as a return to Eden but as a going on to the new creation in which the old will be, not given back as it was, but transformed and fulfilled.

2. We cannot imagine we are living in a world without redemption; so we cannot argue that the evil of which all are aware is omnipresent and all powerful within the present world and that nothing can be done about it.

3. We are not members of Israel BC; so—as one example out of many—we ought not to rebuild the Jerusalem Temple and offer animal sacrifices in it.

4. We are not living during the time of Jesus's public career and must not assume that, for example, the temporary prohibitions on preaching the gospel to non-Jews (Matthew 10:5–6) apply to us. (You can tell that the prohibition is temporary, because it is explicitly lifted after the resurrection, in 28:19. Not all cases are that easy; some are actually very difficult, as we see with Paul's wrestlings over questions of the Jewish law; but there is usually a clue.)

Perhaps we might put it like this. When we read Genesis 1–2, we read it as the first act in a play of which we live in the fifth. When we read Genesis 3–11, we read it as the second act in a play of which we live in the fifth. When we read the entire story of Israel from Abraham to the Messiah (as Paul sketches it in Galatians 3 or Romans 4), we read it as the third act. When we read the story of Jesus, we are confronted with the decisive and climactic fourth act, which is not where we ourselves live—we are not following Jesus around Palestine, watching him heal, preach, and feast with the outcasts, and puzzling over his plans for a final trip to Jerusalem—but which, of course, remains the foundation upon which our present (fifth) act is based. Indeed, telling the story of Jesus as the climax of the story of Israel and the focal point of the story of the creator's redemptive drama with his world is itself a major task of the fifth act, which is why both the oral tradition of storytelling about Jesus and the eventual writing of the canonical gospels in precisely that narrative mode was, and remains, one of the great founding moments of this act.

To live in the fifth act is thus to presuppose all of the above, and to be conscious of living as the people through whom the narrative in question is now moving toward its final destination. When we arrive there, just as there will be no Temple, no sacraments, and even, dare we say, no prayer of the kind we know at present—because all will be swallowed up in the immediate presence and love of God—so there will be no need any more to read scripture, not because it is irrelevant but because it turns out to be the map to a destination we have now reached. That is the point toward which I glance in the final paragraph of this book.

This means—a point of enormous importance in many contemporary discussions—that our relationship to the New Testament is not the same as our relationship to the Old, and that we can say this with no diminution of our commitment to the Old Testament as a crucial and non-negotiable part of "holy scripture." The New Testament is the foundation charter of the fifth act. No change of act in God's drama with the world (despite manifold changes in human culture) has occurred between the time of the apostles and evangelists and our own; there is nothing that would correspond to the great double change of act (from Act 3 to Act 4, and from Act 4 to Act 5) which occurred between their time and that of Torah, Prophets, and Writings. Even granted that the New Testament writers were not (despite frequent assertions) playing fast and loose in their treatment of the Old (pages 52–57), we do not stand over against them in the way they did over against their canonical predecessors.

We who call ourselves Christians must be totally committed to telling the story of Jesus both as the climax of Israel's story and as the foundation of our own. We recognize ourselves as the direct successors of the churches of Corinth, Ephesus, and the rest, and we need to pay attention to what was said to them as though it was said to us. We cannot relativize the epistles by pointing out the length of time that has passed between them and us, or by suggesting any intervening seismic cultural shifts which would render them irrelevant or even misleading. It is an essential part of authentic Christian discipleship both to see the New Testament as the foundation for the ongoing (and still open-ended) fifth act and to recognize that it cannot be supplanted or supplemented. The fifth act goes on, but its first scene is non-negotiable, and remains the standard by which the various improvisations of subsequent scenes are to be judged. That is what it means for the church to live under the authority of scripture—or rather, as I have stressed all along, under God's authority mediated through scripture.

The New Testament offers us glimpses of where the story is to end: not with us "going to heaven," as in many hymns and prayers, but with new creation. Our task is to discover, through the Spirit and prayer, the appropriate ways of improvising the script between the foundation events and charter, on the one hand, and the complete coming of the Kingdom on the other. Once we grasp this framework, other things begin to fall into place.

The notion of "improvising" is important, but sometimes misunderstood. As all musicians know, improvisation does not at all mean a free-for-all where "anything goes," but precisely a disciplined and careful listening to all the other voices around us, and a constant attention to the themes, rhythms, and harmonies of the complete performance so far, the performance which we are now called to continue. At the same time, of course, it invites us, while being fully obedient to the music so far, and fully attentive to the voices around us, to explore fresh expressions, provided they will eventually lead to that ultimate resolution which appears in the New Testament as the goal, the full and complete new creation which was gloriously anticipated in Jesus's resurrection. The music so far, the voices around us, and the ultimate multi-part harmony of God's new world: these, taken together, form the parameters for appropriate improvisation in the reading of scripture and the announcement and living out of the gospel it contains. All Christians, all churches, are free to improvise their own variations designed to take the music forward. No Christian, no church, is free to play out of tune. To change the metaphor back to the theater: all the actors, and all the traveling companies of which they are part (i.e., different churches) are free to improvise their own fresh scenes. No actor, no company, is free to improvise scenes from another play, or one with a different ending. If only we could grasp that, we would be on the way to healthy and mutually respectful living under the authority of scripture.

Strategies for Honoring the Authority of Scripture

How can we be sure that our understandings and "improvisations" of scripture facilitate the Spirit's working in and through us, as individuals, congregations, and the larger church? We do so by a reading of scripture that is (a) totally contextual, (b) liturgically grounded, (c) privately studied, (d) refreshed by appropriate scholarship, and (e) taught by the church's accredited leaders.

So we come to the positive proposals for the ways in which the authority of scripture—i.e., God's authority exercised through scripture—can be the dynamic force within God's people that it is meant to be, energizing them for mission (pages 115–118) and ordering their life accordingly.

A *Totally Contextual* Reading of Scripture

We must be committed to a *totally contextual* reading of scripture. Each word must be understood within its own verse, each verse within its own chapter, each chapter within its own book, and each book within its own historical, cultural, and indeed canonical setting. (There may of course be a tension between the historical setting of part of scripture and the place it now occupies in the complete canon; if so, both should be taken clearly into account.) All scripture is "culturally conditioned." It is naive to pretend that some parts are not, and can therefore be treated as in some sense "primary" or "universal," while other parts are, and can therefore safely be set aside. The doctrine of Jesus's divinity is culturally conditioned: as Paul says, the incarnation happened "when the time had fully come" (Galatians 4:4), and part of that fullness was precisely a culture that would resonate with the new events. The doctrine of justification by faith is culturally conditioned: only within a world already accustomed to notions of God's justice, of the Jewish law, and of the promises to Abraham could such a thing have been conceived. We must read the Bible with as full and clear an understanding of these contexts as we can.

To do so is an enormous, though exhilarating, task. Fortunately, there is more help available for it than ever before: such a variety, in fact, that the beginner may well wonder where to start. (Some suggestions can be found in the Appendix at the end of this book.)

But it is not simply the Bible's context that we must understand. As many have pointed out, it is equally important that we understand and appreciate our own, and the way it predisposes us to highlight some things in the Bible and quietly ignore others. I have already spoken about this when thinking about our present cultural context (see chapter 5) and tradition (pages 118–120).

This contextual reading of scripture is a project which is never finished. We shall never plumb the inexhaustible riches of the text in its own terms, and so we shall always be grateful for advances in lexicography, archaeology, and all the other studies that contribute to fresh insight. (This does not mean that we can never arrive at good answers to difficult questions. Further refinement of scholarship will not lead us, for instance, to question the two doctrines I mentioned a moment ago—the divinity of Jesus and justification by faith—only to understand them better.) Likewise, we ourselves are so different both from one another, individually and globally, and indeed from the people we ourselves were a few years ago, that it is important always to be reassessing our readings and understandings, and taking delight in their development and in watching new insights arise and make themselves at home. A properly contextual reading of scripture will celebrate the rich diversity of material within the canon, resisting attempts to flatten it out into a monochrome uniformity, while at the same time always looking for the larger unity within which different emphases are held together. An appeal to the whole over against some of the parts ("Read the Bible," some have advised, "like drinking beer, not like sipping wine") can be a necessary corrective to a narrow and distorting angle or focus of vision. But it can equally become an excuse for avoiding those parts which happen not to fit with the particular big picture the interpreter is eager to promote.

Such a contextual reading is in fact an *incarnational* reading of scripture, paying attention to the full humanity both of the text and of its readers. This must be undertaken in the prayer that the "divinity"—the "inspiration" of scripture, and the Spirit's power at work within the Bible-reading church—will thereby be discovered afresh. Far too often the ancient conflicts over Jesus's incarnation have been mirrored in debates over the nature of scripture, with "conservatives" stressing divinity and "liberals" or "radicals" stressing humanity. (I know that the analogy between the Bible and the person of Jesus is not exact, and that some have seen serious problems with it; I believe that, provided it is seen *as an analogy,* not as a precise two-way identity, it remains helpful.) Genuine orthodoxy needs both, and in proper mutual relationship.

A *Liturgically Grounded* Reading of Scripture

The primary place where the church hears scripture is during corporate worship. (I shall come to individual reading presently, but I believe corporate worship to be primary.) This is itself a practice in direct descent from the public reading of the law by Ezra, Jesus's own reading of Isaiah in the synagogue at Nazareth, the reading of Paul's letters in the assembled church, and so on. However different we may be personally, contextually, culturally, and so on, when we read scripture we do so in communion with other Christians across space and time. This means, for instance, that we must work at making sure we read scripture properly in public, with appropriate systems for choosing what to read and appropriate training to make sure those who read do so to best effect. If scripture is to be a dynamic force within the church, it is vital that the public reading of scripture does not degenerate into what might be called "aural wallpaper," a pleasing and somewhat religious noise which murmurs along in the background while the mind is occupied elsewhere.

It also means that in our public worship, in whatever tradition, we need to make sure the reading of scripture takes a central place. In my own tradition, that of the Anglican Communion, the regular offices of Morning and Evening Prayer are, in all kinds of ways, "showcases for scripture." That is, they do with scripture (by means of prayer, music, and response) what a well-organized exhibition does with a great work of art: they prepare us for it, they enable us to appreciate it fully, and they give us an opportunity to meditate further on it. The public reading of scripture is not designed merely to teach the people its content, though that should be a welcome spin-off. (The word "lesson" in this context originally meant simply "reading," not "teaching"; its modern meaning throws the emphasis in the wrong direction.)

More, in public worship where the reading of scripture is given its proper place, the authority of God places a direct challenge to the authority of the powers that be, not least those who use the media, in shaping the mind and life of the community. But the primary purpose of the readings is to be itself an act of worship, celebrating God's story, power, and wisdom and, above all, God's son. That is the kind of worship through which the church is renewed in God's image, and so transformed and directed in its mission. Scripture is the key means through which the living God directs and strengthens his people in and for that work. That, I have argued throughout this book, is what the shorthand phrase "the authority of scripture" is really all about.

Indeed, what is done in the classic offices of Morning and Evening Prayer, by means of listening to one reading from each Testament, is *to tell the entire story of the Old and New Testaments,* glimpsing the broad landscape of the scriptural narrative through the two tiny windows of short readings. To truncate this to one lesson, or to a short reading simply as a prelude to the sermon (and perhaps accompanied with half an hour or more of "worship songs"), is already to damage or even deconstruct this event, and potentially to reduce the power and meaning of scripture, within this context, simply to the giving of information, instruction, or exhortation. Equally, to have a reading that lasts about ninety seconds, flanked by canticles that last five or ten minutes (the practice in some "cathedral-style" worship), conveys the same impression as a magnificent sparkling crystal glass with a tiny drop of wine in it. The glass is important, but the wine is what really matters. The systems whereby readings are chosen (called "lectionaries" in some traditions) must be so arranged that ordinary Christian worshippers are confronted, as far as possible, with the *whole* of scripture, especially the whole of the New Testament, on a regular basis.

There has been a tendency in some quarters, no doubt stemming from a desire to keep services from going on too long, to prune the length of readings—and to use that as an excuse for cutting out parts which might not serve as the kind of aural wallpaper people are used to, but might instead shock them into listening with alarmed attention. Many debates within the church have been seriously hampered because there are parts of the foundation text—a verse here, a chapter there—which have been quietly omitted from the church's public life. There is simply no excuse for leaving out verses, paragraphs or chapters, from the New Testament in particular. We dare not try to tame the Bible. It is our foundation charter; we are not at liberty to play fast and loose with it.

The sermon, which from early in the church's life was seen as primarily an exposition of or reflection on scripture, belongs of course very closely with the public reading of scripture—not, to repeat the point, that scripture is read only in order to be preached upon, or that there is only one style of scriptural preaching. Indeed, this is one of the points at which "Act 5" comes into its own. Precisely when scripture is read in the way I have described, all kinds of opportunities will arise for fresh words to be spoken, illuminating the passages that have been heard and reverberating with them, but also moving forward to suggest what fresh meanings they might bear for today and tomorrow.

Finally, of course, the reading of scripture during the Eucharist, at the very center of the church's life, witness and worship, is the crucial thing that forms God's people *as* God's people as they come together solemnly to "proclaim the Lord's death until he comes." Within that, it becomes a vital part of the personal formation of each individual communicant. Scripture forms God's people, warming their hearts as with the disciples on the road to Emmaus, so that their eyes may then be opened to know him in the breaking of the bread.

A *PRIVATELY STUDIED* READING OF SCRIPTURE

For all this to make the deep, life-changing, Kingdom-advancing sense it is supposed to, it is vital that ordinary Christians read, encounter, and study scripture for themselves, in groups and individually. The famous passage about the inspiration of scripture in 2 Timothy 3:16–17 was written, not so much to give people the right belief *about* scripture, as to encourage them to study it for themselves. Western individualism tends to highlight individual reading as the primary mode, and liturgical hearing as secondary, encouraging an Enlightenment-driven fragmentation of the witness of the whole church; by reversing this order, I do not for a moment mean to downgrade the importance of private reading. Study at all levels, with others and by oneself, is part of the church's continual calling to listen more closely to scripture as a whole and in its parts. Indeed, scripture is a key means by which we can grow, as we are bidden, in loving God with our mind (through study) and with our heart (through devotional reading). It forms part of that complex pathway whereby each Christian is simultaneously called to worship and prayer, supplied with fresh understanding, puzzled by new questions (and so stimulated to yet more study and questioning), and equipped to take their own place in the ongoing story of God's people as they engage in his mission to the world. This is precisely what the authority of scripture looks like in practice, day by day and week by week, in the life of the ordinary Christian—and *all* Christians are ordinary Christians.

There is an important spin-off to this point. If it is part of the privilege and duty of each Christian to study scripture, and to read it devotionally, it is important that the wider church should be able to hear what individual readers are discovering in the text. Of course, not all private readings will come up with significant new insights; but many will. The church needs to facilitate, through small groups and other means, this bringing of particular viewpoints to the attention of the whole body, both so that the larger community may be enriched and so that maverick or clearly misleading readings can be gently and appropriately corrected.

A READING OF SCRIPTURE *REFRESHED BY APPROPRIATE SCHOLARSHIP*

Biblical scholarship is a great gift of God to the church, aiding it in its task of going ever deeper into the meaning of scripture and so being refreshed and energized for the tasks to which we are called in and for the world. Many churches, including my own, have retained the Reformers' emphasis on the "literal sense" of scripture, not in the sense of "taking everything literally" but in the sense of "discovering what the writers meant" as opposed to engaging in free-floating speculation. As I pointed out earlier, the "literal sense" means the sense originally intended; thus, ascertaining the "literal sense" of a parable involves recognizing it *as* a parable, not an anecdote about something which actually happened. Getting at the original sense of scripture is an ongoing task for scholar, preacher, and ordinary reader alike.

Biblical scholarship needs to be free to explore different meanings. This is not just the imperative of the modern scholar, always to be coming up with new theories in order to gain promotion or tenure in the university. It is also a vital necessity for the church. Any church, not least those that pride themselves on being "biblical," needs to be open to new understandings of the Bible itself. That is the only way to avoid being blown this way or that by winds of fashion, or trapped in one's own partial readings and distorted traditions while imagining that they are a full and accurate account of "what the Bible says." At the same time, however, biblical scholarship, if it is to serve the church and not merely thumb its nose at cherished points of view, needs to be constrained by loyalty to the Christian community through time and space. When a biblical scholar, or any theologian, wishes to propose a new way of looking at a well-known topic, he or she ought to sense an obligation to explain to the wider community the ways in which the fresh insight builds up, rather than threatens, the mission and life of the church.

Such a statement will provoke protests—some of which will simply indicate that the protesters are still living within the modernist paradigm, and pretending to an illusory detached "neutrality." Of course, the church has sometimes gotten it wrong, and tried to demand of its scholars an adherence to various forms of words, to ways of putting things, which ought themselves to be challenged on the basis of scripture itself. The Christian "rule of faith" does not, in fact, stifle scholarship; even if it provokes the scholar to try to articulate that rule with greater accuracy and elegance, that itself will be a worthy task. Those who try to cut loose, however, discover sooner or later that when you abandon one framework of ideas you do not live thereafter in a wilderness, without any framework at all. You quickly substitute another, perhaps some philosophical scheme of thought. Likewise, those who ignore one community of discourse (say, the church) are inevitably loyal to another (perhaps some scholarly guild, or some drift of currently fashionable ideology).

What loyalty means is, in my experience, better discovered in practice than by hemming one another in through ever more carefully worded dogmatic statements which reflect ever narrower definitions within particular traditions. The Bible is a big enough book, and the church ought to be a big enough community, to develop a relationship of trust between its biblical scholars and those involved in the many other tasks to which we are called. True, that trust has been sorely tried in the last few generations. Sometimes the tension between scholarly freedom and loyalty to the community has become unbearable. Some scholars have cut loose from the church, or come up with theories which appear to mock what most Christians have cherished. Many in the church have turned their back on serious study, and have embraced an anti-intellectualism which refuses to learn anything from scholarship at all lest it corrupt their pure faith. It is time to end this stand-off, and to reestablish a hermeneutic of trust (itself a sign of the gospel!)

in place of the hermeneutic of suspicion which the church has so disastrously borrowed from the postmodern world. The framework I have sketched is designed to help toward a reconciliation and integration of the different and mutually supportive facets of the church's life.

A READING OF SCRIPTURE *TAUGHT BY THE CHURCH'S ACCREDITED LEADERS*

Finally, we must encourage and enable a reading of scripture that is *taught by the church's accredited leaders*. (The word "leader" is actually not very helpful for various reasons, but I use it here as a summary of the various offices listed in Ephesians 4:11 and elsewhere.) This obviously includes people at several different levels of ministry, including for instance those who take charge of Sunday schools and home groups. But, in my tradition, it means bishops in particular; and perhaps it is at that level that certain things need to be said.

It might seem obvious that church leaders should be teachers of scripture, but today it is by no means necessarily so. All too often the official leaders of the various denominations are so swamped with bureaucratic and administrative tasks that, though they still preach sermons and perhaps even give lectures, they do not give the church the benefit of fresh, careful, and prayerful study of the text, but rather simply draw on their studies of many years ago, and the inspiration of the urgent moment. When this happens, the problem is not merely that the church will miss out on new insights, and be treated to the recycling of well-worn ideas. The real danger is that church leaders forget *what "the authority of scripture" actually means in practice.* And if that happens, the chances are that that authority will not be working as it ought to be.

As I have argued in this book, "the authority of scripture" is really a shorthand for "the authority of God exercised through scripture"; and God's authority is not merely his right to control and order the church, but his sovereign power, exercised in and through Jesus and the Spirit, to bring all things in heaven and on earth into subjection to his judging and healing rule. (Ephesians 1 sets this out more spectacularly than most passages.) In other words, if we are to be true, at the deepest level, to what scriptural authority really means, we must understand it like this: God is at work, through scripture (in other words, through the Spirit who is at work as people read, study, teach, and preach scripture) to energize, enable, and direct the outgoing mission of the church, genuinely anticipating thereby the time when all things will be made new in Christ. At the same time, God is at work by the same means to order the life of the church, and of individual Christians, to model and embody his project of new creation in their unity and holiness. To be a leader in the church is, almost by definition, to be one through whose work this mission comes about, enabled and directed by this scripture-based energy; and one through whom, again with scriptural energy to the fore, that unity and holiness is generated and sustained.

If, therefore, those called to office and leadership roles in the church remain content merely to organize and manage the internal affairs of the church, they are leaving a vacuum exactly where there ought to be vibrant, pulsating life. Of course Christian leaders need to be trained and equipped for management, for running of the organization. The church will not thrive by performing in a bumbling, amateur fashion and hoping that piety and goodwill will make up for incompetence. But how much more should a Christian minister be a serious professional when it comes to grappling with scripture and discovering how it enables him or her, in preaching, teaching, prayer, and pastoral work, to engage with the huge issues that confront us as a society and as individuals. If we are professional about other things, we ought to be ashamed not to be properly equipped both to study the Bible ourselves and to bring its ever-fresh word to others.

The teaching and preaching of scripture remains, then, at the heart of the church's life, alongside and regularly interwoven with the sacramental life focused on the Eucharist. (This book is not about the sacraments, but in case anyone suspects me of highlighting the word at the expense of the sacrament, let me point them to my little book *The Meal Jesus Gave Us* [Westminster John Knox, 2002].) The balance between what can be said in a sermon and what must be said in non-liturgical teaching, adult education, and so on, will vary from church to church and place to place. It is fair to say that most churches, even those with well-developed educational programs, have a long way to go in their teaching of scripture. It is also important to remind preachers that, just as some of the Reformers spoke of the sacraments as God's "visible words," so sermons are supposed to be "audible sacraments." They are not simply for the conveying of information, though that is important in a world increasingly ignorant of some of the most basic biblical and theological information. They are not simply for exhortation, still less for entertainment. They are supposed to be one of the moments in regular Christian living when heaven and earth meet. Speaker and hearers alike are called to be people in whom, by the work of the Spirit, God's word is once again audible to the heart as well as to the ears. Preaching is one key way in which God's personal authority, vested in scripture and operative through the work of the Spirit, is played out in the life of the church.

When we explore this dynamic meaning of "the authority of scripture," we realize in a new way that the "authority" of accredited church leaders cannot consist solely or primarily of *legal structures,* important though both church structures and canon law are in their own ways. It must be primarily, as it was with the apostles, a matter of *proclaiming the word in the power of the Spirit.* The Western church has for some generations allowed a dangerous "separation of powers," according to which scripture is taught by professional academics while the church is run by clergy who, with noble exceptions, rely on secondhand and increasingly outdated understandings of scripture itself. (Not that the latest scholarship is always the best; if more teachers in the church were schooled in the works of Lightfoot and Westcott we would be better off!) The result is not only a deep impoverishment, but a creeping or even galloping bureaucratization, as church leaders engage in displacement activities, hoping to do through committees, filing cabinets, and legal constraints what they should be doing through prayerful, powerful biblical preaching, teaching, and pastoral work. As Professor Oliver O'Donovan said when preaching at an episcopal consecration not long ago,

> The bishop, though not without . . . legal powers, needs to be able to call upon an authority with deeper springs than any statutory power. He needs an authority that comes straight from the presence and working of God the Holy Spirit in our midst. . . . It is the riskiest and the greatest of all ventures of authority, but the one that most attests the nature of the church.

The church of the first three centuries would hardly have recognized the models of Christian leadership into which we, at least in the modern Western churches, seem to have slipped without anybody much noticing. Nor do these models sit well with any claim, in whatever mode, to "apostolic" office. Of course, bishops and other church leaders will not be the only teachers. Excellent full-time scholarship and instruction remains an essential resource. Teaching must go on at every level. But if bishops and other church leaders are not teachers of scripture, able to lead the church thereby in its mission to the world and order its internal life to reflect God's unity and holiness, then "the authority of scripture," in the senses explored above, is simply not functioning. The various crises in the Western church of our day—decline in numbers and resources, moral dilemmas, internal division, failure to present the gospel coherently to a new generation—all these and more should drive us to pray for scripture to be given its head once more; for teachers and preachers who can open the Bible in the power of the Spirit, to give the church the energy and direction it needs for its mission and renew it in its love for God; and, above all, for God's word to do its work in the world, as, in Isaiah's vision, it brings about nothing short of new creation— the new world in which the grim entail of sin has at last been done away:

> For as the rain and snow come down from heaven,
> And do not go back there until they have watered the
>   earth,
> Making it fertile, making it sprout,
> Giving seed for the sower and bread for the eater,
> So shall my word be that goes forth from my mouth:
> It shall not return to me fruitless,
> But it shall accomplish my good pleasure,
> And succeed in the purpose for which I sent it.
> For you shall go out in joy and be led forth in peace;
> The mountains and the hills will break into joyful
>   shouts before you,

And all the trees of the field shall clap their hands.
Instead of the thorn shall come up the cypress;
Instead of the brier shall come up the myrtle.
It shall make a name for YHWH,
an everlasting sign that shall not be cut off.

Isaiah 55:10–13

9.

Case Study: Sabbath

The theory is one thing. What happens when we try to think through some more specific issues in the light of all that we have said so far? I choose two quite different topics: sabbath and monogamy. Both of these have been controversial from time to time, but neither is currently a "buzzing" issue; had they been, it might have been tricky to discuss them without appearing to push a particular agenda and so slant the theory as well. Studying these two questions will challenge some of the oversimple readings of scripture which have been all too popular, and illustrate the overall point of the present book about a more mature way to read scripture, a way to treat it as a genuine vehicle of God's authority.

The first question is that of the sabbath. Here the biblical evidence is very striking. In the Old Testament, the sabbath command is solid, fierce, mandatory. It is rooted in the two greatest narratives which shaped ancient Israel: Creation and Exodus. Sabbath is appropriate because God rested on the seventh day after completing his creative work. It is commanded because God brought Israel out of Egypt. Bad things happen when the nation or individuals within it ignore or override the sabbath. Fresh sabbath observation will bring Israel to a new place of favor (Isaiah 56:4–7). Loyal Jews in the last few centuries BC made sabbath keeping one of the major distinctive marks, to the point where one of the few things the average pagan knew about the strange Jewish people living in their midst (along with circumcision and the food taboos) was that they had a lazy day once a week. The question of whether Jews were allowed to defend themselves on the sabbath became pressing when enemies, spotting a chance, chose that day to attack. (The modern equivalent was of course the Yom Kippur war of 1973, when the enemies of the State of Israel launched their attack on Yom Kippur, the day of atonement.)

But in the New Testament, all that has changed. I shall come back to Jesus and the gospels in a moment. But our earliest Christian writer, Paul, is remarkable in what he says about the sabbath: more or less nothing. The two other major issues for Jews in the pagan world are there in his letters, indeed sometimes front and center: Do Christians need to get circumcised, and are Christians obliged to keep the Jewish food laws? No and no, answers Paul; indeed, to insist on circumcision for Gentile converts is to draw them into the physical family of Abraham, not the one true, renewed people of God formed in and around the Messiah, Jesus. That is what the letter to the Galatians is all about. Likewise, any attempt to restrict fellowship on the basis either of what you eat or of who you eat it with is firmly, not to say fiercely, ruled out. But the sabbath?

Well, there are a couple of passages where Paul may have it in mind. In Romans 14:5–6, he says that some Christians like to observe special days, and others are happy not to, and that those who do shouldn't judge those who don't, and vice versa. More sharply, in Galatians 4:10 he denounces those who are observing "days, and months, and seasons, and years." That might be a reference to Jewish festivals in general—obviously going a lot wider than just the sabbath—but it isn't clear from this what precisely Paul *would* have said about the sabbath itself. Or why.

This interesting question—something so central in Jewish life, which Paul, Jewish to his fingertips, doesn't even deal with in passing—is sharpened further when we look at the times when Paul quotes the Ten Commandments themselves, in which of course the sabbath commandment plays a prominent role. At the very points where he is saying that followers of Jesus are obliged, in the Spirit, to keep the commandments, he manages to omit the sabbath from the list (e.g., Romans 13:9). No murder, theft, adultery, or coveting; honor your father and mother; and of course, behind all that, worship the one true God, and honor and sanctify his name. But the sabbath is nowhere to be seen.

Of course, when we come to Jesus and the gospels, the sabbath is frequently highlighted—and Jesus always seems to be falling foul of it. There is a well-known story of a church in the Scottish highlands where strict "sabbath" observance was the norm. One day the elders were discussing the matter, and one of them pointed out that Jesus had repeatedly broken the sabbath and had spoken out against its observance. "Ah yes," replied another. "It really seems that even our blessed Lord himself was a bit of a liberal on that matter."

But is that all we can say about it? Was it the case, as one well-known scholar suggested a while ago, that Jesus was a "radical" and Paul a "liberal"? Or is there a better, deeper, more scripturally satisfying explanation of what's going on? To answer this we need to look in more detail at how the sabbath commandment plays out in the two testaments in turn, with Jesus poised as it were in between them. Is this simply a case where the Old Testament commands something which the New Testament abolishes? If so, how do we explain this flat contradiction? Is it because the New

Testament has overturned the "legalism" of the Old with a new "religion of grace"? Or are we faced with a different sort of question altogether?

The Scottish discussion I mentioned a moment ago reminds me of the Oscar-winning movie *Chariots of Fire*. The plot was constructed around the 1924 Paris Olympics, which ended with Eric Liddell winning the 400 meters and Harold Abrahams the 100 meters. But Liddell had originally been entered for the 100 meters. He had, famously, refused to take part in the heats because they were to be run on a Sunday. The hidden irony of the film was that Liddell, the devout Christian, was the one who took the principled Sabbatarian position, whereas Abrahams, the Jew, had no apparent difficulty about events taking place on Saturday, the Jewish sabbath.

Liddell's stance represents the way things were in much of Britain, at least, until sometime around the 1960s. I remember as a boy in the 1950s not being allowed to play outside in the street on Sundays. All shops were shut, except briefly in the morning for newsagents selling Sunday papers. Few cafés or restaurants were open. Public transport ran on a very limited schedule. There was no professional sport. All that has gone now, of course, and opinions differ as to whether the change is altogether for the better. The main push for a different way of doing Sunday seems to have come from the big shops, eager for another day to make money (though keeping the shops open an extra day doesn't create more spending money in the pockets of the public). But the main argument advanced—very similar to other arguments put forward in favor of other secularizing agendas—was about the inappropriateness of a Christian restriction about the sabbath being imposed on a society that had either abandoned Christian faith or never had it in the first place, and most of whom certainly weren't going to spend their Sundays going to church or church-related activities. Despite the best efforts of the Keep Sunday Special campaign to demonstrate the broad, general human principles about a rhythm of work and rest, it always felt, to most people in Britain, like a bunch of Christians trying to shore up an outdated and irrelevant practice. For many people, it appeared that the Christians, already determined to be miserable or at least bored one day a week, wanted everyone else to be miserable or bored as well.

But who said that Sunday, the first day of the week, was the Christian sabbath anyway? How come Christians so effortlessly switched the ancient Israelite law about the seventh day of the week to a similar law about the first day, without seeming to worry about the large hermeneutical step that was being taken—or about the apparent clash with the teaching of Jesus and Paul?

That is a complicated question for the historians to puzzle over. Opinion has come and gone. When I was editing the works of the early English Reformer John Frith, I discovered that the edition of his writings that most people used, which was published forty years after his untimely death, had omitted one line from his original text. Frith lived and worked in the heady days of early Reformation, when all kinds of rules that were perceived as medieval Catholic "legalism" were being swept away. When it came to the keeping of Sunday, he insisted that the New Testament left one free: once one had been to worship, the rest of the day could be spent in any way one wanted. Forty years later, the more cautious editor who pulled together most of his works in the Elizabethan period simply didn't want to print what Frith had written. He omitted the whole sentence. Was that a reinvention of "legalism"? What was going on in terms of the authority of scripture itself—the principle to which both Frith and his later editor claimed to adhere?

Where do we start if we are to get at these issues? Well, the obvious place to begin is the Old Testament material itself.

Sabbath in the Old Testament

That basic principle of the sabbath is stated clearly enough in Genesis 2:3. But what it actually says there, though outwardly simple, is actually deeply mysterious and pregnant. God finished the work of creating the heavens and the earth on the sixth day, and then "rested" on the seventh day. What does this mean?

For a start, it appears to mean that God, having created a world which includes "time" itself, the forward movement of the world and events within it, is somehow himself within, or at least in relation to, this time which he has created. God creates a world of space, time, and matter; declares that it is very good (so that we would be wrong to see space, time, and matter as somehow second-rate, shabby things); and then, as it were, takes control of it, not being bound by the relentless need always to be working, to be creating. Creation is going somewhere. It is a project, not a tableau or a machine. It contains a rhythm within which God's own rhythm of life somehow seems to be intersecting mysteriously with ours.

One way of understanding this has been proposed, on the basis of detailed study of comparative material in the ancient Near East, by John Walton in his remarkable book *The Lost World of Genesis One*. Walton insists that in that ancient world anyone reading about something being built by a god in six days or stages would know that it was basically a *temple,* a dwelling for the god himself or herself. And what the god would do after the six days of construction was not simply to stop working and have some time off. The god would enter the newly constructed house and "rest" there—in the sense of "taking his ease," taking up residence and being at peace in his new home. This gives quite a new perspective on the Genesis sabbath institution. If Walton is right, it has to do with the creator's enjoyment of his world, his celebration of heaven and earth as a dwelling for himself.

As with a Temple, the final part of the whole operation is when, with the structure just about complete, an image of the god himself is inserted into the shrine. This "image" will then, as it were, face both ways: it is the mode and means of the god's presence in the house, and it is the focal point of the homage and devotion which the god will receive. So here in Genesis the human pair, male and female, are the mode and means of the creator's presence in his newly made world, and the ones through whom the rest of creation is brought into fruitful order. And the image-bearing pair themselves are called to share in the creator's enjoyment of his world, by themselves keeping sabbath. What the creator does, his image bearers will also do. They will "take their rest" together.

The idea of God the creator "taking his rest" after completing his work implies, too, that God will then continue to work, to take forward his great project. This is in sharp contrast (for instance) to Deism, in which the creator sits back and takes no further part, allowing creation to run on under its own steam. The grain of truth in this, of course, is that the creator *has* made plants and animals that produce "seed" and so reproduce themselves, and that the humans, in particular, are appointed as the creator's agents to bring order and fruitfulness into the world. But we shouldn't take this as a hint that the creator himself is permanently absent or inactive. These, rather, are the ways in which he has chosen to work. He has made a world which is itself full of creative energy. The usual modernist either/or, in which *either* God "does something" in the world *or* events come about by "natural causes," is fundamentally misconceived. The "natural causes" are themselves the result of God's underlying creative activity.

The sabbath plays no apparent role throughout the rest of Genesis, but it returns with a bang in the book of Exodus. There, even before the giving of the Ten Commandments in chapter 20, the story of the manna in chapter 16 incorporates a clear sense of the

six-day rhythm of life. This is then amplified in the (to us) shocking story of the man in Numbers 15:32 who collects sticks on
the sabbath and who is stoned to death for his pains. The commandment itself is linked to creation in Exodus 20:8–11, and then,
interestingly, to the Exodus itself in Deuteronomy 5:12–15, where
the point being made is that Israel, having experienced the transition from slavery to freedom, must be sure to give slaves themselves
their own moment of freedom every sabbath. The sabbath thereafter does not occur as a major theme for much of the rest of the
Old Testament. Interestingly, though, it emerges in the exilic and
postexilic period as a sign of God's call for renewed loyalty from his
people. And where it does occur, it is mentioned in such a way as to
imply that everyone basically knows what the sabbath is and why,
with the only question being whether they keep it or not (Nehemiah 13:15–22; Isaiah 56:2–7; 58:13–14; Jeremiah 17:19–23—where
the promise for sabbath keepers includes the renewal of the monarchy). (See too, Exodus 23:12; 31:13; 34:21; 35:2; Leviticus 19:3; 23:3;
Numbers 28:9; Nehemiah 9:14; Ezekiel 20:13; 22:26; 44:24.)

So the picture of the sabbath we get from the Old Testament is
of a commandment which is important as much for what it points
to as for its actual observance. It is a sign that the created order is
going somewhere. Creation, as I said, is a *project,* not a tableau or a
machine. Sabbath indicates a rhythm of life in which God's own
rhythm of life mysteriously intersects with that of humans, of Israel,
and of the whole creation. Sabbath is thus the *temporal* sign of the
creator's interaction with the creation, as the Temple becomes the
geographical sign: "to profane the sabbath" (e.g., Ezekiel 20:13; 22:8,
26; 23:38) is analogous to profaning the Temple itself. We arrive at
this rule of thumb: *as Temple is sacred space, so sabbath is sacred time.*

The two themes meet, of course, in Israel's great festivals. These
were partly harvest festivals, partly historical recollection of the

Exodus events. These often incorporated special sabbaths, "great sabbaths," in which time itself was mysteriously folded back on itself: the obvious example, Passover, is the moment when the Israelites not only *remember* the time when God liberated them from Egypt, but also actually *recapitulate* it: "this is the night." At such moments, space, time, and even matter (the food and drink of the Passover meal) are all transcended and brought together in new ways, not because creation is inadequate but because it is designed to point forward, beyond itself, to the time when the creator's purposes are complete.

Within this, a major theme emerges in which the sabbath principle and command find a new focus, though with echoes of the Deuteronomy principle (sabbath as liberation for the slaves). The sabbath becomes the sign of God's justice and care for the poor, and even for slaves and animals. Thus, in Exodus 23:11, the sabbath is the chance for the poor to rest; this includes slaves and animals too. This principle blossoms, importantly, into a theme which looks quite different to begin with but actually belongs very closely with the sabbath: the Jubilee.

The Jubilee is the remission of debts in the seventh year, and the great Jubilee is the large-scale version of that after every forty-ninth year (seven times seven, of course). This principle is stated in Leviticus 25. There is to be a "sabbatical year" every seven years (25:1–7), in which the land itself is to enjoy rest. But then, after forty-nine years (seven times seven, referred to as "seven weeks of years"), the blast of a trumpet will announce "liberty throughout the land to all its inhabitants." Ancestral property is to be restored, thus creating a special law about buying and selling land (one buys or sells a certain number of harvests running up to the next Jubilee). This even applies to the buying and selling of slaves, once again with a reference to Israel's time as a slave in Egypt (25:47–55).

During the land's sabbaticals the people are to eat what the land produces of itself.

But the greatest statement of Jubilee is found in Isaiah 61. There, following on from the insistence on sabbath observance in Isaiah 56 and 58, we come to the announcement of liberty to the captives, sight to the blind, and so on. The point of the Jubilee is basically to restore God's creation and God's people—to put things right in human society, human bodies, human lives, and the land which they cultivate. The sabbath principle is thus intimately related to the large principle of God's *justice* in the sense of God's intention— which itself is part of a theology of creation—to put all things right at the last. The Jubilee appears to be a moment of "sacred time" when humans are privileged to share in God's time *and God's redemptive purposes*. It is the gift of the creator to his people, particularly to the poor and the enslaved: the gift of justice itself. It is interesting that as the Western world has eroded the notion of Sunday observance to its vanishing point (though I shall later suggest that Sunday observance was often based on a misunderstanding), so the idea of justice for the poor, of a redemptive remission of debt, has disappeared as well.

The principle of Jubilee, a kind of multidimensional sabbath, is itself given a fresh dimension in the book of Daniel. Daniel, in exile in Babylon, knows that Jeremiah had prophesied that the exile would last for "seventy years" (Jeremiah 25:11; 29:10; Daniel's prayer in chapter 9, the reference to Jeremiah being at 9:2; see also 2 Chronicles 36:21; Zechariah 1:12; 7:5). Daniel prays that he may know when these seventy years will be concluded and exile at last undone. The angel who responds to him brings good and bad news: redemption will indeed come, but instead of seventy years it will be "seventy times seven," four hundred and ninety years: a kind of Jubilee of Jubilees. This appears cognate with the notion that the exile was a way of allowing the land of Israel to "enjoy its sabbaths," the sabbaths that the greedy inhabitants had denied it in their eagerness for gain (Leviticus 26:34, 43; 2 Chronicles 36:21). The land itself needs a rest from relentless exploitation; exile and return are not just a mere surface punishment for Israel's idolatry but a sign that God will provide the sabbath rest that is needed and will thereby restore his people and the whole creation in the proper way. We thus have a sabbath principle woven into larger history—a sense that God will work in patterns which have "new creation" inscribed on them. Justice for Israel and the world, for humans and creation, are not merely a repeated symbolic pattern. God will eventually give them, and give them completely, as a one-off event.

The sabbath in the Old Testament is thus far more complex as an institution and symbol than might at first appear (and that has appeared when people have read scripture merely in search of "commands to obey"). It is about much more than merely the command to abstain from work on the seventh day of the week. It appears to be about (among other things) a call to humility and hope—the humility of recognizing that work (which for most meant working the land) was not the be-all and end-all of life, a frantic, relentless greed. Like tithing, and particularly like the offering of fine animals as sacrifices, the keeping of the sabbath was a stepping back from the idea that Israel, or human beings, actually owns or runs the world. Overwork, working seven days a week, correlates with a loss of faith in God the creator and provider. And the sabbath was also about hope—the hope that God would keep his promises, and that through the cycles of linear time he would bring about the ultimate "rest," the equivalent of his own "enjoyment" of creation at the beginning and of Israel's "rest" in the land after the conquest. (The Land, and within it the Temple, are then to be seen as foretastes of God's claim on, and desire to dwell within, the whole world.) This principle of looking ahead to the time of redemption was to be instantiated in Israel's national life through the fifty-year cycles, which were signposts to the larger redemption of all creation, and which were themselves anticipated in the weekly rest. The alternative, threatened by Jeremiah, is that creation would lapse back into *tohu wa'bohu,* "without form and void," the condition of chaos that preceded the original creation (Jeremiah 4:23, referring to Genesis 1:2).

If we are to understand what happens to the sabbath in the New Testament, it is vital to keep this whole larger picture in mind. To truncate the ancient biblical picture of the sabbath into merely a rule or law to be rigorously imposed and blindly obeyed—and then to hail Jesus or Paul as the great antilegalist!—is first to trivialize, then to misunderstand, and finally to ignore the real significance of the sabbath principle first in ancient Israel and then in the great renewal which Jesus launched and Paul implemented.

We might well think, once we understand the complex, intricate, and interlocking principle of sabbath in the Old Testament, that it might be a good thing simply to continue with it. I am no farmer, but I suspect modern agriculture might be a lot better if the sabbath were observed. But the New Testament has something else in mind. In Jesus, God is doing a new thing.

Sabbath in the New Testament

As we saw earlier, the strangest thing about the sabbath in the New Testament is its near absence. The other nine commandments are, in their various ways, reaffirmed; but not this one. What's more, Jesus and Paul both appear to challenge the sabbath observance of first-century Jews head-on. The Son of Man is Lord of the sabbath; the sabbath was made for doing good, not harm. For this, and the accompanying actions, plots are hatched on Jesus's life (Mark 2:23–28; 3:1–6; and parallels Luke 13:10–17). In John, the initial healing of the man at the pool of Bethesda (John 5:1–18) causes anger and threats, which are reemphasized after the healing of the man born blind (John 9:1–17). These two healings on the sabbath, on top of the synoptic stories, have given rise to the long-running interpretation according to which the Pharisees, with their insistence on sabbath observance, were "legalists," and Jesus was challenging them to a different sort of religion: a religion of the heart and of grace, instead of a religion of outward observance and human self-effort. More recent scholarship, with a deeper understanding of first-century Judaism, has frequently observed that this does scant justice to the way in which most Jews then, and in many cases since, have actually viewed the sabbath both as an institution and in practice. Not least for those whose daily life and work have been hard or even harsh, the seventh day has provided much-needed and welcome rest and refreshment. To reiterate the earlier point: there was, and has remained in Judaism, a sense of the sabbath as sacred time in the same sense that the Temple was sacred space. Sabbath is seen as a time when God's time and human time overlap and intersect, so that one might sense time in a different way, with a different quality, as one does with great music.

So why would Jesus so pointedly cut a swath through this great and God-given institution? The only explanation which will do— but it will do very well indeed—is that Jesus believed he was inaugurating the new age *toward which the entire sabbath institution had been pointing*. He had come to announce and enact the Jubilee of Jubilees, the sabbath of sabbaths, the time when God's purposes and human life would come together at last. His actions in relation to

the sabbath are thus the exact analogue of his actions in relation to
the Temple, about which I have written elsewhere. Jesus acted as if
he were the Temple in person, offering people forgiveness on his
own authority; thus, when he came to Jerusalem, a clash was inevitable as he confronted the existing Temple and its authorities with
the reality to which they were supposed to be pointing but which
they had in fact perverted. This analogy suggests that, with the sabbath as well, Jesus may well have had a sharp critique of the actual
interpretation and (unofficial) "enforcement" of the sabbath by at
least some of the Pharisees. (The Pharisees were an unofficial pressure group; but, then as now, unofficial or self-appointed guardians
of public behavior have ways of persuading people to follow their
system.) But the underlying point is the *eschatological claim* that Jesus
was making: "the time is fulfilled; God's kingdom is at hand!" The
fulfilment of time indicates that the project which God the creator
began in creation, and the redemptive project launched in the
exodus, had reached their destination. Israel's destiny, humankind's
destiny, creation's destiny were being realized in Jesus. His bodily
presence was the reality to which the Temple pointed; his human
lifetime, more specifically his short public career, was the moment
when God's time and the world's time overlapped and intersected.
That, at least, was the implicit claim—which seemed absurd and
scandalous to many at the time, and seems so still. Jesus's followers
insisted that the claim had been made good in his resurrection,
which carried its own sense of new time. Especially in John's treatment, "the first day of the week" symbolizes the launch of the new
creation.

The most explicit statement of the long-awaited fulfillment of
time is found in the famous "Nazareth manifesto" in Luke 4:16–30.
Here Jesus evokes Isaiah 61, which as we saw itself looked back
to the Jubilee legislation in Leviticus: he was the one who would

usher in the time of good news to the poor, liberty to captives, and
so forth, and this was the time when it would happen. "Today,"
he said, "this scripture is fulfilled in your hearing" (Luke 4:21).
That didn't just mean "Fancy that! Here's a verse of scripture being
fulfilled!" in the sort of miscellaneous sense that one might comment on the prediction of some political commentator coming
true. Rather, it meant that the whole of Israel's history, and with
it the whole of cosmic history, had reached its ultimate Jubilee—a
time of freedom and peace not only for Israel but also, as became
dangerously apparent in Nazareth that day, for the whole world.

Right away there was a clash of expectations and meanings. Jesus
was clearly not fulfilling the aspirations of many of his contemporaries who wanted a straightforward act of political liberation.
(His kingdom announcement had no effect on the imprisonment
and execution of his cousin John the Baptist.) But, through acted
symbol and explicatory parable, he stuck to his message: this was
indeed the time for which Israel had longed, even though it did
not look like what most of his contemporaries had expected.

But if this was the time of fulfillment, then it was inappropriate to go on emphasizing the advance signposts, the weekly sabbaths, in a way which suggested that the time of fulfillment had
not arrived. "The Son of Man is Lord of the sabbath": one does
not put up a sign pointing toward London in Piccadilly Circus.
Jesus seems to have chosen, quite deliberately, to speak and act
in such a way as to communicate the message that, through his
healings in particular, God's time of liberation had arrived. This
was the moment when God's time and human time, God's saving
power and broken human lives, would intersect at last. "Come to
me," he said, "and I will give you rest." For people to refuse to see
this, and to insist on continuing as before with regular sabbath
keeping, would be, in effect, like someone insisting on continu-

ing to plough the field at the very moment when the crop was beginning to come up. The sabbath was not a silly, unnecessary, or trivial institution (as many Christians, reading the gospels in a quasi-Marcionite fashion, have supposed). Still less was it about a Pelagian kind of moralism, a system of "good works" whereby one might earn God's favor, "good works" which could then be fine-tuned in accordance with the regulation-bound mentality to which all societies are subject from time to time. Like most other things in ancient Judaism, the sabbath was a forward-looking sign. When the reality arrived, not only was the sign no longer needed. It had the potential to become a dangerous distraction from the new Fact. To go on looking at the alarm clock to see whether it is morning yet when the risen sun is flooding the bedroom with golden light is perverse. The whole early Christian movement was predicated upon the belief that in Jesus that new Fact had arrived at last, and that the advance signposts, though properly God-given to that point, were now redundant.

This explains, quite straightforwardly, the absence of sabbath ful-fillment in Paul. "When the time had fully come," he writes in what may be his earliest letter, "God sent forth his son, born of a woman, born under the Law, to redeem those under the Law" (Galatians 4:4). Those who receive this redemption are "God's children," and upon them God sends "the Spirit of his Son." They have, by this means, "come to know God—or rather, to be known by God," and as a result must no longer be bound by the days, months, seasons, and years which mark out ancient Jewish time and also, of course, ancient pagan time. Thus "the fullness of time" in Galatians 4:4 rules out the careful observance of time markers in Galatians 4:10. The same logic underlies the dismissal of sabbath observance and other Jewish festivals in Colossians 2:14–16. Equally, when faced with the challenge of drawing together Christian groups from different backgrounds, Paul can treat the sabbath as merely indifferent. Some keep it, some don't, and neither group should pass judgment on the other (Romans 14:5–6).

This latter point (treating the sabbath as *adiaphoron*, something over which one should not divide the church) can be allowed only once the basic principle has been massively affirmed—that in Jesus the Messiah, God's new day has dawned. "Now is the acceptable time," writes Paul elsewhere; "now is the day of salvation" (2 Corinthians 6:1–2, quoting Isaiah 49:8). The "but now" of Romans 3:21, and the strong note of fulfillment all through Romans 3—8, creates a context in which one can then relax and allow for variation in practice. But inside this principle a further theme emerges from an unexpected angle. Paul insists that now, in this new day that has dawned, "works" are not the way by which God's people are marked out. *Justification by faith alone is, as it were, a new radicalization of the ancient sabbath.*

This connection is made explicitly in the letter to the Hebrews, which envisages the entire new age inaugurated by Jesus as a great "sabbath rest," and speaks of those who "enter God's rest" ceasing from their "works." The whole sequence of Hebrews 3:7—4:11, especially the final verses of that sequence, provides an exegesis of Psalm 95:7–11, in which the story of the wilderness wanderings, and of Joshua leading the people into the promised land, is evoked in terms of a promised "rest," which Joshua clearly had not provided and which the Psalm holds out as a still-future possibility.

When we reach Romans 8, where creation itself is set free from its bondage to decay to share the freedom which comes when God's children are revealed, we realize that all along the great biblical narrative, with the regular sabbaths as the way markers, has been about the project of Genesis 1 and 2 reaching its final intended conclusion, having overcome on the way the destructive entail of sin. This is the goal to which the sabbaths had pointed. This goal, the renewal of all things, is already given in principle in the resurrection of Jesus from the dead. God's sovereign rule over the world and God's "righteousness" as his faithfulness both to creation and covenant come together in the fulfillment of sabbath and Jubilee alike. This is the ultimate freedom moment, the completion of the "new temple" in which God and humans alike will "rest," will be at home.

John's gospel presents the same theme in a quite different mode. The well-known sequence of "signs" that runs through the gospel reaches (arguably) its seventh and climactic moment when Jesus dies on the cross. The old creation, and the old covenant, is complete. We are now to await the dawning of the new creation. This is symbolized by John's emphasis on the "first day of the week" in John 20:1. This sends us back to the day of Jesus's crucifixion, the sixth day of the week, on which God created humans in his own image, the day on which Pilate declares "behold the Man" (19:5). That is when Jesus dies, with the word *tetelestai,* "it is completed," echoing the statement of completion at the end of the first creation account (19:30; Genesis 2:3). After that comes the "rest" of the seventh day, the sabbath, when Jesus is in the tomb. Then, of course, comes the first day of the week, the day of resurrection, which John takes care that we should not miss, repeating the point morning and evening (John 20:1, 19). Once we factor into this the way in which Jesus in John explains that "my father is working still, and I am working" (5:17), we reinforce the sense that Jesus himself is the fulfillment of the sabbath, as he is (in John, rather obviously) of the Temple, and that God's time, as well as God's space, has converged on him. The new creation which is launched in his resurrection is a sustained divine/human time, not one moment alone, or a succession of moments, but a continuing quality of time. We shall explore this further a bit later.

The book of Revelation likewise structures itself in a complex series of sevens. But when the new heavens and new earth are unveiled in chapter 21, we discover that all the signposts that pointed forward to this moment fall away once the reality itself is there. Not only is there no Temple. There is no sun and moon and no night. Endless day, it seems, is the result—in the light of "God and the Lamb." Not only is this the "place" which, by the personal presence of God and the Lamb, is the reality to which the Temple pointed. This is also the "time" toward which the repeated sabbaths had pointed. When the perfect is come, the partial is done away.

With all this in mind, we should not be surprised that the early church celebrated the first day of the week as "the Lord's day." Jesus had inaugurated the new creation, and the start of every week now made this point in a way which any adherence to the Jewish sabbath simply could not. Paul expects the Corinthian Christians to meet together on the first day (1 Corinthians 16:2); this pattern appears again in Acts (20:7), and the first day of the week is referred to in Revelation 1:10 as "the Lord's day" without further explanation. We should remind ourselves that the first day of the week was, of course, an ordinary working day for everyone in the ancient world, pagan and Jew alike. The Christians, by meeting on that day (presumably very early, before work began), were symbolically enacting Jesus's victory over death itself. Various subapostolic and second-century writers explore the notions of time and sabbath, but it is fair to say that this is not a major preoccupation of the period.

The reminder that "the first day of the week" was, and remained, a normal working day in all parts of the ancient world tells us something else too: the early Christians show no signs whatever of trying to transfer the basic principle of sabbath observance, namely, the cessation of normal work, to this new day. It would in any case have been totally impractical, except perhaps where an entire household had converted and the master might give the slaves the day off. But the Christians did do various things which would previously have seemed impractical, and there is no hint of them trying to force the point on this one. The ordinary business of life had to go on, and we find no early Christians complaining that they were being forced to collude with pagan ways, or indeed campaigning to be allowed to keep "their" new day in the way the Jews kept their old one. The apparent transfer of "sabbath" to Sunday took place much later.

Sabbath, Time, and Christian Hope

It would be easy, too easy, to say that the old institution of the sabbath has been transcended in the Christian dispensation, as though Judaism had given way to Platonism and the whole idea of significant time had itself been swept away in favor of a timeless vision, a timeless gospel, a timeless word from a God outside time, summoning us to forget the world of time and enter into God's nontemporal eternity. This would, I repeat, be too easy, though many in the Western Christian world have gone that route. Sometimes, indeed, it has been combined with the "normal" view that sabbath keeping was legalistic and that the early Christians were simply antilegalists because they believed in a more "spiritual" religion. This simply won't do as a serious account of what we find in the New Testament; and it certainly won't do as an attempt to discover what it might mean to regard scripture as "authoritative" in this area.

We seem to be faced, rather, with something altogether more complex and interesting. Linear time (which was part of God's good creation) continues, but it is now intersected with a new phenomenon, a new kind of time. This is not what T. S. Eliot called "the intersection of the timeless with time," but rather the intersection of two different kinds of time. In God's time, events from the past and the future can, and sometimes do, come together. Just as in one sense the Exodus is recapitulated in Jesus's death (as it was in another sense recapitulated in every Passover), and the new creation itself is anticipated in his resurrection, so time seems now capable of being telescoped together and then pulled apart again. One might even call this "Spirit-time": Acts speaks of the day of Pentecost "having fully come," *symplērousthai,* and in Leviticus (23:5–21) Pentecost itself is a form of Jubilee, a moment when time is concentrated together into a celebration of God's gift of himself in the Torah.

All of this is focused on the person of Jesus himself, and it seems (to be frank) as though the modern Western preoccupation with either proving or disproving something called "Jesus's divinity" has blinded the orthodox and the radical alike to themes which, for the early Christians, were clustering around Jesus and providing a grid of "meaning" much more dense and evocative than the rather flattened out Western categories of "divinity" and "humanity." For the early Christians, Jesus was the new Temple—in other words, the place where, and the means by which, heaven and earth came together. For them, too, I have been suggesting, Jesus's ministry, death, and resurrection were the new Jubilee—the *time in which* God's liberating purposes came at last to intersect with human life, generating a permanent state of Jubilee. In addition, though this is a whole separate topic, Jesus *in his physical body, crucified and risen,* turns out to be the material substance in whom, as Paul puts it, "all the fullness of divinity dwells bodily." All this is then true, as well, by and through the Spirit, in and through those in whom the

Spirit dwells. Here, I suggest, we have something much, much bigger than simply the question of whether "Sunday" is "the Christian sabbath," with new antiwork regulations to match. We are, rather, faced with the redemption and transformation of space, time, and matter themselves, in and through Jesus and then in and through his Spirit. There is no way back from here into old-style Sabbatarianism, however much Christian legalists of various sorts (both Papist and Puritan, for the record) have wanted to create such a thing. That would at best be a distraction from the much more exciting and important task of exploring and implementing the good news that with Jesus and the Spirit *a new way of being,* a new mode of creation, a new way of being *human,* has been launched upon the world.

What, then, happens to linear time itself? Some have suggested, in an inappropriate rush of Platonic blood to the head, that it should cease to matter, so that history itself would become a dangerous distraction for the Christian. But the picture of the new creation we find in Revelation 21 and 22 tells a different story. Here, in the new heaven and new earth, we have a picture of a new creation which contains a new *project.* "The leaves of the tree are for the healing of the nations" (Revelation 22:2), and the whole scene seems to be a place, not of static "rest" in the sense of idleness, but of fresh, vibrant life, celebration, and fruitful work. Insofar as there is a "rest" after this life, Revelation places this as the time in between human death and resurrection, not as the final state (Revelation 6:11; 14:13). What happens in the end is not "rest," but "reign": the rule of God's people over God's world, while being of course the adoring subjects of God himself and the Lamb (see details in my book *After You Believe*).

This brings us back to the notion of time as still linear but now intersecting in various ways with other schemes of time, so that the ongoing sequence of ordinary time is shot through with both memory and anticipation, with ancient events becoming contemporary and future events coming forward into the present. This, I think, is what Augustine was talking about in his explorations of memory and imagination. And I suspect, too, that this may be what contemporary physics, at least since Einstein, have been groping after—a sense screened out by the modernist paradigm of straightforwardly linear time and three-dimensional space, but which is now making something of a comeback. Perhaps our world really *is* far more complicated than we have realized. And perhaps our forebears in faith were aware of that and were expressing that multidimensional complexity in symbols and imagery which we have treated as marginal but which we are now in a position to recall....

It is, after all, paganism that wants either to divinize creation or to marginalize it. Suppose there is a different way? Suppose creation is after all made to be the dwelling of God himself, and of ourselves as God's image-bearing creatures, and that creation itself, made to be filled with the knowledge and glory of God as the waters cover the sea, is capable of telling this story, even in advance, as Psalm 19 seems to suggest? Suppose, in other words, that the universe is in some sense *sacramental*—not fully, not yet, because the final redemption is still awaited and the danger of an overrealized eschatology is as real here as anywhere else. But perhaps, as Gerard Manley Hopkins saw, the world is already "charged with the grandeur of God," already pregnant with the future glory which the present corruption has hidden but not removed? Suppose the sabbath was a true signpost, a pointing forward to a time not only of rest but also of glory, a time when God would be at home in his creation and the creation at home with God? This speaks of a transformation of space, time, and matter, a transformation which sacramental theology does its best to monitor but which it scarcely generates out of nothing.

Again, the picture of God's ultimate future in Revelation 21 and 22 offers rich insights. Just as there will be no Temple in the city, so (as we saw) there will be no sun or moon. There will, it seems, still be something we can call time, because there will be projects, work to do, leaves on the tree for the healing of the nations, kings of the earth bringing their treasures into the city. Whatever these rich symbols mean in relation to that ultimate reality, they are certainly not speaking of a static entity, not even like the final chord of a symphony held on and on forever. There is new music in the new world.

My central point in this section, then, is that the sabbath command of the Old Testament was a true and necessary signpost, pointing forward to God's purposes for his creation and to the place of Israel in relation to those purposes. But it was always, from the perspective of Genesis 2:3, a sign which spoke of God coming to live in his heaven-and-earth creation, taking up residence, dwelling in the midst of his people. In the gospels, the actions of Jesus on the sabbath thus speak powerfully of his belief that "my father is working still, and I am working." Sabbath is a sign of eschaton to come; the New Testament speaks of Jesus acting as if he were the eschaton in person, sacred time come to life. This, I suggest, rather than any simplistic "rejection of legalism" or any such thing, is what lies behind the wholesale disappearance of the sabbath command in early Christianity. And this is the clue to the way in which the surprisingly complex scriptural material about the sabbath can be powerfully authoritative for the Christian in our own day, or in any day.

Sabbath Today?

Where does this leave us in terms of the keeping of the sabbath? And what have we learned about our underlying topic, the "authority of scripture," or rather, God's authority exercised through scripture?

For a start, our investigation makes the repetition of the Ten Commandments, as they stand, quite problematic. Church members have long been able to screen out things like "I am the Lord your God who brought you out of the land of Egypt," hearing that great claim merely as a pleasant metaphorical preamble (and perhaps linking it to the paschal events of Jesus's death and resurrection). But have they been able to "decode" the sabbath command? I suspect not. It may be, indeed, that the inclusion of the full ten commandments in Christian liturgy, despite the New Testament's noninclusion of the sabbath command, has had something to do, down the years, with a Christian sabbatarianism which has assumed, without question or irony, that "the Lord's Day" now accrues to itself all the meaning of the seventh-day legislation in the Old Testament.

So is there no "Christian equivalent" to the Old Testament sabbath? Well, yes, I suggest there is. But it works quite differently. Now that heaven and earth have come together in Jesus Christ, and now that the new day has dawned, we live (from that point of view) in a perpetual sabbath. "The time has fully come," and we should not try to downplay the note of realization, of a new sort of time already launched. So perhaps the proper way to celebrate any kind of "Christian sabbath" would be just that—a celebration: a way of recognizing in creative ways, in music and art and dance and family life, the fact that heaven and earth have indeed come together in a new way in Jesus, that the "rest" of the old sabbath has been replaced by the "celebration" of the new.

This view of time is cognate with a Christian view of space (or "place") and matter. The fact that the "new Temple" has been established in Jesus and by the Spirit does not mean there is not a proper Christian theology of sacred space. The fact that all creation has now been hallowed in a new way through the Son of God becoming part of our clay-made humanity does not mean that there are not particular elements of creation which he himself taught us to hallow as modes of his presence and love—in other words, water, bread, and wine. In addition, again according to Jesus himself in Matthew 25, we should add to these the poor and needy: when we treat them well or ill, he said, we are doing it to him. All these, then, are new forward-looking signposts to the coming reality. So, too, places where Jesus is known, honored, and invoked in prayer, sacrament, and service become signposts to the complete filling of earth with his glory. The sacramental elements borrow from that future glory-filled creation to convey the presence and power of Jesus even in the present time. In the same way, we recognize two apparently clashing realities. Yes, the time has fully come, but still "the days are evil" (Ephesians 5:15–16; Colossians 4:5). Time both *has been* redeemed and transfigured and *is yet to be* redeemed fully. That is why we are commanded to "redeem" it even in the present. Any fresh Christian appropriation of elements of the sabbath must be seen within this larger picture.

Here we need to draw on wider reserves of wisdom. A healthy human life will always take account of God's purposes for creation, for animals, for the poor and the exploited. We need in particular to figure out appropriate ways in which this new sort of time, fulfilled and yet still to be redeemed, a time in which God's presence is known in a new way, can best be marked. It seems to me, in fact, that the early Christians, long before they thought of "translating" the old sabbath into the new Sunday, were marking the Lord's Day in one thoroughly appropriate way, by celebrating together the meal which spoke of his victorious and time-fulfilling death. And the Lord's Day might be thought of, around that central act, not in terms of things *not* to be done but rather of undertaking specific things that it is good and appropriate to do, not of refusal to do certain types of work so much as of determination to do certain other types—acts of healing, of mercy, of creativity, of justice, of beauty, of love. These things may well be different from the things we do in the rest of the week. Sunday is, in many cultures, an excellent day for people to visit prisons, to volunteer to help in a local hospice, to give time to elderly or housebound neighbors, and to enable disadvantaged children to find fresh air and a wider supportive family. All such things would symbolically remind us of the coming together of God's time and our time in Jesus Christ, while pointing to the fully redeemed time yet to come.

This presupposes, however, that a wise ordering of all human life is already taking place, in which the peculiarly modern Western preoccupation with relentless work has been firmly put back in its place. We need, perhaps, to reimagine a contemporary meaning for the command in Deuteronomy that farmers should not glean their fields to the edges, but should leave something for the poor and the animals. Farm buildings where birds could formerly nest under the eaves are becoming less bird-friendly; hedgerows which used to house thousands of small animals and insects are being cut down to create larger fields, with no thought for the unintended consequences in the larger ecosystem. And so on. In our world there is too much work for some, and not enough for others, which has to be a bad sign. Things are becoming dangerously unbalanced, as some stay in their offices well over twelve hours a day while others lounge at home, or on the streets, with nothing to do. A wise use of time would be part of a program to address this imbalance. Much of the relentless overuse of time stems, after all, from a nervous anxiety about resources: I must do a bit more work, to make a bit more money . . . and the fresh use of the Lord's Day which I am proposing might only "work" if the other six days of the week are themselves balanced in terms of work and rest. All of this might be an "application," not only of the sabbath principle in general, but of the Jubilee principle in particular. Now that Jesus has announced and enacted the Jubilee, one of the greatest things any Christian can work for is precisely release from debt. I have written elsewhere about the need to write off the massive and ridiculously unpayable debts of many of the world's poorest countries. I did not expect to see a time when governments around the world would suddenly agree to write off the debts *of extremely rich banks*. Jubilee today for the rich, and tomorrow for the poor if they are lucky! This is a world out of joint, a world that urgently needs to recapture the deep heart of the message of Jesus.

In particular, if the "rest" of Genesis 2 is the moment when God comes to "inhabit" the home he has built, the Temple which is heaven and earth, so there is a lot to be said for the celebration of the home, whether large or small, as the place simply to be, to be occupied in small-scale but creative and contented domesticity. Certainly if anyone were to hear my suggestions about Sunday as yet another nail in the coffin of the home life of the already overbusy Christian, the whole structure I am proposing would be undermined.

What I am saying, then, is that there is not, and could not be, a straightforward "transfer" from the Old Testament sabbath to the Christian Sunday. Nor is the apparent abolition of the former anything to do with "Jewish legalism," or a slackening of God's absolute and complete demand on his human creatures. Rather, the gospel of Jesus Christ turns the sabbath, like everything else, inside out. It gives us back responsibility: What are *you* going to do this Sunday that is creative, that brings justice and mercy, that offers healing and hope? This is the typical, characteristic Christian stance of seeing all God's promises finding their "yes" in Jesus Christ, and then working out, riskily, what that is going to mean in practice. We may well get it wrong. Here, as elsewhere, we have to "be transformed by the renewal of our minds," and as that Spirit-given process takes effect, we learn not least from our mistakes. But even the mistakes are taken up in the comedy of grace—just as our continuing linear time is shot through, punctuated, and infested with God's past events of creation, exodus, and above all Jesus, and with God's future event of the renewal of all things, the judgment and mercy through which the whole creation will finally be put to rights.

What has all this taught us about reading the Bible and living under God's authority by doing so? Several important things, I believe.

To begin with, it is abundantly clear that we cannot simply scoop up all sorts of "commandments" from the Old Testament and assume that they can be applied as they stand following the resurrection of Jesus from the dead. But this is not, emphatically not, because the Old Testament was a lesser revelation, a shabby first attempt to get a message through to us, from which things then "progressed" to "better" things later on as people started to catch on and the message became less distorted (with the implication that maybe by now we have advanced still further and can leave behind some of the New Testament as well!). That sort of reaction comes about only because, for many in the Western world and church, the Bible is thought of basically as a kind of rule book, with the only questions being, What are the rules, and How shall we apply them? The Bible is much, much more than that (though not less; "rules," or rather the guidelines within which Christian character is to be formed, remain important, even though without the larger biblical context we will not understand why they are what they are or how to work with them: see *After You Believe*.) The Bible, as I have insisted throughout this book, is a *story,* and its authority is put into operation when we learn how the story works and where we belong within it. In terms of the five-act play, the Old Testament sabbath law is a vital part of Act 3, rooted indeed in Act 1 itself. But when Act 4 brings in a new day, Act 3 is seen, not as a sidetrack or backwater, but as the necessary but time-limited step by which the ground is prepared for that fresh fulfillment. And we who live in Act 5 must go on telling the story of all five acts in order to understand the abiding significance of sabbath, albeit translated into the life-giving "now" of the gospel. Merely to treat the Old Testament sabbath command as an ancient and restrictive rule now happily abolished would be to ignore the entire principle which Jesus massively affirmed in Luke 4 and elsewhere: God intended to come in person to live within his creation, within its space, time, and matter, and when he did so his prime task would be to bring liberty to captives and, not least, release from debt.

Once again, then, we see how shallow and misleading it would be to think of the authority of scripture in terms of some (earlier) parts as teaching a religion of self-help moralism, with the sabbath as a prime example of an arbitrary commandment, the observance of which would somehow earn God's favor, so that the "authority" of the New Testament would be its trumping the old by abolishing such a demeaning way of life. The old standoff between "legalism" and "antilegalism" simply misrepresents where the main biblical issues lie. Rather, there is a great transition marked by Jesus himself and his death and resurrection, and we must read the whole Bible in the light of that and not assume that we can ignore it and draw general principles at will from either testament without relation to him. As we saw, the authority of scripture is a function of the authority of Jesus himself.

But this great transition doesn't mean we can then ignore the Old Testament. On the contrary, we understand what the New

Testament means only by reference to the Old, to the narrative and symbol which were the God-given pointers to what was to come. To read scripture like this is to affirm it all, from Genesis to Revelation, as what it is, not as what it is not: the story whose climax is Jesus Christ, the open-ended story into which we ourselves are enfolded, the story of heaven and earth made one, of God and humankind made one, of time past and time future enfolded into the single present of Jesus Christ, so that now all time is transformed by his presence. We are called to live in the endless sabbath of God's new creation, even while the old creation continues to groan in labor awaiting its full redemption. The latter continuing condition (the groaning of creation) means that we still need to order our lives wisely with an appropriate rhythm of work and rest, to be navigated and negotiated case by case and from place to place, and most likely honoring the seven-day rhythm of creation in some appropriate fashion. But the former condition—and if we don't recognize this condition, the already-inaugurated endless sabbath of God's kingdom, we are like the muddled Galatians, wanting to go back to the apparent security of rules designed for the period "before faith came"—means that the old seventh-day sabbath of Exodus and Deuteronomy has completed its work. That is both the explanation for Jesus's otherwise strange actions and sayings. It is also the clue to how the authority of scripture actually works in this particular case. The nighttime candles are made redundant by the rising sun. The very phrase "authority of scripture" only works properly when it points, as scripture obviously does, beyond itself—to the real-time, real-world story of creation and covenant which reached its climax in Jesus himself and which now reaches out into the world with the message of freedom and rest, the sabbath message the world is still hungry to hear.

10.

Case Study: Monogamy

My second "worked example" of how scripture mediates the authority of God concerns the initially unlikely question of monogamy—the lifelong marriage between one man and one woman.

I say "initially unlikely" from a modern Western perspective. In that world, many outside the church as well as inside it will be surprised that the question should even be raised. I am of course well aware that there are many parts of the world where polygamy is allowed and even encouraged. I originally wrote the phrase "to this day" in that sentence, but that is a bit of a giveaway: the idea that family morality has been steadily "advancing" to the point where previously "primitive" forms of life are being left behind is precisely one of the patronizing assumptions that regularly prevents us Westerners from thinking clearly in such matters. Thus English newspapers expressed surprise, curiosity, and not a small ethnic superiority-complex when, early in 2010, the president of South Africa came to pay a state visit to Her Majesty Queen Elizabeth, bringing with him one of his several wives. They (the wives) seemed happy with the arrangement. He, when asked, insisted that in his own culture polygamy had been and still was the norm. Since even bigamy (having merely two wives) is illegal in Britain, as in many parts of the modern Western world, polygamy is multiply illegal. Something of a curiosity, in fact.

Such a perspective would itself seem peculiar, and once more patronizing, in many parts of today's world. In fact, it is a well-known problem among Christians in some countries, including many traditional societies and some predominantly Muslim countries: What does a man do if he becomes a Christian but already has three wives? Divorce is forbidden him, but so is polygamy. The solution of some African Christians has been to say that such people may become Christians, that they are not required to abandon all but one of their wives (in many cultures, that would be desperately cruel), but—this is important—that they will not be ordained. And any children of polygamous converts must not themselves become polygamous, unless they wish to abandon the Christian faith the parents have embraced.

The world is, in fact, far more complex and confusing on these matters than many Westerners realize. Of course, in America itself, as is well known, the Mormons have made their case, and live their own lifestyle. But that is regarded by most other Americans as raising a question, not offering an answer.

So far as I know, hardly anyone else in the modern Western world has challenged the assumption that monogamy is to be regarded as a norm. True, there is at the moment a move in some parts of America toward polyamory, an arrangement in which three or more persons of either sex agree to share one another's lives, including sexual relationships of various kinds. This appears to be a looser version of polygamy, a combination—at least in principle—of polygamy and bisexuality, of polygyny (one man, many wives) and polyandry (one woman, many husbands). But for most people in this modern world, monogamy is still assumed to be the norm. Those who want to live out other options normally go the route either of clandestine affairs or of divorce and remarriage, rather than attempting to increase, by fair means or foul, the size of the basic married unit. Love triangles are, alas, common; ménages à trois less so.

I suspect that most people would, if asked, justify the norm of monogamy with reference to the Judeo-Christian tradition. But why? Where in the Bible does it say that marriage should always and only be between one man and one woman? Are not some of the great heroes of scripture notable for their multiple marriages, from Jacob with his two wives (and two extras) to David with his few dozen, to Solomon with his few hundred? Where in the New Testament does it say that this won't do anymore? I suspect it is only the social context in the Western world that has stopped more people from remarking on this, and on the issues of biblical interpretation and authority that are raised by it. It is the issues of biblical authority that concern us in this book, but we must get our heads around the actual topic to see what "biblical authority" might actually mean in this case.

After all, within living memory a very large majority in the Western world believed much the same about homosexual behavior as most people still do about polygamy: this was a strange practice which "we" did not condone. How times have changed. And in the continuing debate about homosexual behavior, those who have supported the "newer" liberalization have poured scorn on books such as Leviticus where the most obvious ancient prohibitions are found. Leviticus, after all, prohibits the eating of pork and shellfish; it bans the wearing of clothes made from two or more different materials; it contains all kinds of quasimedical rules and regulations which today's scientific medicine appears to render redundant. So why (runs the argument) should we pay any attention to its codes of sexual conduct? And—here comes the crunch, the implicit assumption behind a great many contemporary ways of misreading the Bible—the Old Testament was in any case a religion of law, of fierce prohibitions, of strict regulations, but the New Testament offers a religion of grace, of regulations relaxed and prohibitions set aside, an "inclusive" world where all sorts of things previously forbidden (pork, shellfish) are now permitted, and all sorts of things previously mandatory (circumcision, sabbath) are now optional. That perception of "how the Bible works" has become endemic in a good deal of today's Western world and church. So when, in the case of monogamy, it appears that the Old Testament is itself far more "liberal" than modern Western custom, what's the problem? If Jesus's message is about inclusivity, why not include people whose instincts run to multiple simultaneous partners? If the New Testament normally relaxes tight Old Testament restrictions, in the interests of a generous, law-free, open-minded, and openhanded inclusivity, how much more should Jesus's followers be prepared to recognize the propriety, the value, the "naturalness," of the multi-marriages which were apparently common in the Old Testament and are never explicitly prohibited in the New?

The case of monogamy shows just how wrong that whole approach actually is. Precisely because the topic has not been a major focus of recent discussion, it serves as a very interesting test case of what "the authority of scripture" might actually mean in practice.

Not, of course, that the Old Testament is full of polygamy. Adam and Eve may have been dysfunctional in other ways, but, even if merely for lack of other options, they are at least married only to each other. But a few generations later we meet Lamech, who has two wives, Adah and Zillah. Lamech is a violent man, taking multiple vengeances on enemies, and it appears that the writer of Genesis disapproves of this (Genesis 4:23–24). But the fact of his having two wives appears to pass with a shrug of the shoulders.

Well, we might say, but that was a wild, lawless time, before God called his people Israel into being. Surely once that people is properly launched, such muddles with the order of creation will be sorted out? Well, they will and they won't. The start is not promising. After nearly a century of monogamous marriage to Sarah, Abraham branches out, at Sarah's own suggestion, and takes her serving maid Hagar as a second wife—only to find that, when she bears him a son, this causes all kinds of new problems. The narrator of Genesis may well be trying to tell us something at this point, but if so, it remains somewhat hidden.

The next generation sees the solidly monogamous marriage of Isaac and Rebecca. I am always gently amused that, in the Marriage Service in the 1662 Book of Common Prayer, we find Isaac and Rebecca woven into one of the prayers as a fine example of faithful monogamy. Whoever composed that prayer was treading on dangerous ground, granted what happened in the generations on either side of Isaac and Rebecca. Abraham, as we just noted, would hardly have served the purpose well. And Isaac's two sons are just as bad: first we find their older son, Esau, marrying two Hittite women who make life bitter for his parents (Genesis 26:34–35). Then of course there is Jacob, who acquires two wives by accident and then two more (their respective serving maids) by design. Again, it may be that the narrator wants to tell us, as the great story of Joseph unfolds—Joseph being Jacob's first son by Rachel, his favorite wife—that all this is very foolish and will end in tears. It does and it doesn't: "you meant evil against me," says Joseph in the end to his brothers, "but God meant it for good" (Genesis 50:20).

So does that mean that the Old Testament is prepared to allow bigamy or polygamy, not necessarily as the best way but as allowable alternatives? So it might seem as the story continues. Indeed, the Mosaic code legislates for the possibility:

If a man has two wives, one of them loved and the other disliked, and if both the loved and the disliked have borne him sons, the firstborn being the son of the one who is disliked, then on the day when he wills his possessions to his sons, he is not permitted to treat the son of the loved as the firstborn in preference to the son of the disliked, who is the firstborn. He must acknowledge as firstborn the son of the one who is disliked, giving him a double portion of all that he has; since he is the first issue of his virility, the right of the firstborn is his. (Deuteronomy 21:15–17)

A similar passage is found in Exodus 21:7–11, appearing to legislate for the possibility that a man may buy a slave girl as a wife and then take a subsequent wife as well, in which case "he shall not diminish the food, clothing, or marital rights of the first wife" (21:10).

The evidence continues in the same direction, with the monarchy increasing it dramatically. Samuel's father has two wives and navigates the tricky line between the one he loves more, who is childless (until the arrival of Samuel) and the one he loves less, who has children (1 Samuel 1:1–28). When we reach David, however, polygamy begins to take off in a big way. Saul has already given him his daughter Michal as a wife (1 Samuel 18:20–29), but this doesn't last long because David has to run away from Saul. David then takes Abigail, widow of Nabal, as a new wife (1 Samuel 25), and, as though incidentally, "Ahinoam of Jezreel" (1 Samuel 25:43). Then, after the death of Saul, he retrieves Michal, despite her hav-

ing been given to another man after he had left home (2 Samuel
3:12–16)—a sad story, reflecting, we may presume, dynastic strategy (not wanting Saul's daughter to produce a rival royal house)
rather than either fidelity or love. It isn't long before they have a
row which leads to David putting a curse on her, resulting in her
remaining childless (2 Samuel 6:20–23). In any case, once David
has been established as king, he does what other ancient potentates
(and some modern ones) regularly did and do: "in Jerusalem, after
he came from Hebron, David took more concubines and wives; and
more sons and daughters were born to David" (2 Samuel 5:13).

Then, of course, not satisfied with all the wives and concubines he can acquire by apparently legitimate means, David crosses
another bridge: adultery and murder. Bathsheba is added to the
large number of his wives, while her brave and noble husband is
lured to his death (2 Samuel 11).

It is this adultery, rather than his polygamy, which the narrator indicates, not simplistically but through the dynamic of the
whole narrative, as the cause of David's subsequent disasters. Moral
corruption at the top spreads through the house, and David's son
Amnon rapes his half sister Tamar (2 Samuel 13), leading to Absalom's murder of Amnon and then Absalom's rebellion, the height
of which is that he, Absalom, goes in to his father's concubines in
a tent on the palace roof (the place from which David had first
glimpsed Bathsheba: 2 Samuel 11:2 with 16:22), in full public view.
David's humiliation is complete, and even though the rebellion is
quashed, and he returns to rule, nothing is ever the same again.
There is a gentle irony in the fact that, when David is very old and
his courtiers think to revive him with a new young concubine, no
sexual relations take place (1 Kings 1:1–4).

The narrator does not seem much to mind the fact that David
has had more wives than most other Israelites. (Indeed, the limit

would seem to be set only by the capacity of a man to provide for such a growing household.) It was adultery, not polygamy, that was the problem.

And it was polytheism, rather than polygamy, that was the perceived problem with David's successor, Solomon. His early marriage to the daughter of the Pharaoh of Egypt (1 Kings 3:1; 9:16) was later supplemented with many other marriages to foreign women, against the example of his father and against the (usually assumed later) command of Deuteronomy 7:3–4. Here the narrator is blunt and to the point:

King Solomon loved many foreign women along with the daughter of Pharaoh: Moabite, Ammonite, Edomite, Sidonian, and Hittite women, from the nations concerning which the Lord had said to the Israelites, "You shall not enter into marriage with them, neither shall they with you; for they will surely incline your heart to follow their gods;" Solomon clung to these in love. Among his wives were seven hundred princesses and three hundred concubines; and his wives turned away his heart. For when Solomon was old, his wives turned away his heart after other gods; and his heart was not true to the Lord his God, as was the heart of his father David. For Solomon followed Astarte the goddess of the Sidonians, and Milcom the abomination of the Ammonites. So Solomon did what was evil in the sight of the Lord, and did not completely follow the Lord, as his father David had done. Then Solomon built a high place for Chemosh the abomination of the Ammonites, on the mountain east of Jerusalem. He did the same for all his foreign wives, who offered incense and sacrificed to their gods. (1 Kings 11:1–8)

We may raise our eyebrows at the idea of David following the Lord completely, but what seems to be meant is that David, though obviously sinning against the Lord and knowing perfectly well he had done so, never worshipped other gods. But here, obviously, we have the primary biblical source for serious polygamy: Solomon, the wisest man in history! There are multiple ironies here, too many even to mention, let alone explore.

These famous biblical polygamists are not, of course, the only ones. A casual Internet search revealed a website (www.biblical polygamy.com) suggesting that the practice of polygamy is somehow "biblical," and listing as "biblical polygamists" (some by implication rather than actual statement) Abdon, Abijah, Abraham, Ahab, Ahasuerus, Asher, Belshazzar, Benhadad, Caleb, David, Eliphaz, Elkanah, Esau, Ezra (not the main biblical Ezra, but an earlier one), Gideon, Heman, Hosea, Ibzan, Issachar, Jacob, Jair, Jehoiachin, Jehoram, Jerahmeel, Joash, Lamech, Machir, Manasseh, Mered, Moses, Nahor, Rehoboam, Saul, Shaharim, Shimei, Simeon, Solomon, Terah, Zedekiah, and Ziba. Some of these are clearly contentious; it is not obvious, for instance, that the Cushite (i.e., Ethiopian) woman whom Moses had married, according to Numbers 12:1, was not in fact the same woman as the Zipporah, daughter of Reuel, whom Moses had married in Exodus 2:21—or, indeed, if the Cushite women was someone else, that Zipporah had not died in the meantime. But the list is quite impressive—for anyone who supposes that if something is "in the Bible" that automatically validates it. The website in question also points out that the Old Testament portrays YHWH himself as polygamous, being married to both Israel and Judah (Jeremiah 3:6–14; Ezekiel 23:4). We might of course retort that a metaphorical picture, as in Jesus's parable of the Unjust Judge, must not be pressed for exact theological claims, but it is indeed striking that the prophets were not shy of such imagery. The same website also notes that when Paul confronts the incestuous man in 1 Corinthians 5, it is assumed that "his father's wife" is someone other than his mother, and draws the conclusion that the father in question had at least two wives. Again, he might have been widowed or divorced and remarried, but let us allow the point to stand for a moment. The website is clearly pushing a line, and doing so with more ingenuity than plausibility; but the evidence must be taken into account.

The question that must be raised through all of this, in a book on the authority of scripture, is: So what?

Here we are close to one particularly important point about scriptural authority. The Bible describes a great many things, tells a great many stories, and sketches a great many characters that are not intended to be examples of how to behave. That ought to be obvious; but if all that counts is "it's in the Bible," we have simply flattened down any kind of serious Christian (or indeed Jewish) reading of the text into the idea that the Bible is a kind of ragbag of helpful hints. This is the nemesis, at another stage of the argument, of the idea that the main point of the New Testament at least is to chronicle "early Christian experience," as though such "experience" is the main thing that matters and anything which will enable people to approximate to it, to recover the initial enthusiasm of Jesus's first followers, is to be welcomed, and even to be treated as authoritative. That, I submit, is a quite radical mistake; and simply to catalog all biblical polygamists, as though that contributed toward such a point, falls into the same trap.

But if Abraham, Jacob, David, and Solomon—four of the undoubted heroes of the Old Testament—were certainly and unchallengeably polygamous, and if the narrator, while drawing our attention to consequent problems, does not condemn them for polygamy as such, on what grounds can we say that a serious Christian reading of the Bible does not in fact support polygamy?

Well, but what about the New Testament? It appears that by the time of Jesus, polygamy had largely died out in Jewish circles (that itself is an interesting question, but not for now). But it was still fairly widespread in some pagan cultures, including of course the cultures from which many early Gentile converts came. That, presumably, is the background to the prohibition on officeholders in the church having more than one wife (1 Timothy 3:2; Titus 1:6) and on the church's official list of widows including any who have had more than one husband (1 Timothy 5:9). But why the prohibition? It seems to imply two things: first, there were some in the church who had been, or were still, polygamous; second, the early Christians believed that the church, through its official representatives, had to maintain a line, and that the public face of the church should bear witness to monogamous marriage and celibacy as the only two allowable options.

Why?

To put off the answer for another moment, it is clear in other related areas, too, that in this department the New Testament is far stricter than the Old. There is no implication of the Old Testament setting up a stringent law and applying it legalistically, and then the whole thing being swept away by the new religion of grace, forgiveness, inclusivity, or whatever. On the contrary. In the Old Testament divorce is easy (though one of the later prophets declares that God hates it: Malachi 2:16); in the New Testament, it is forbidden except under very stringent and particular circumstances (Matthew 5:32; 19:9; 1 Corinthians 7:8–17). In my view, these passages allow for remarriage after such divorce, but there are serious scholars who disagree. In the Old Testament celibacy is not noted as a serious option, and in the world of the New Testament the same would have been true; almost everyone married. But in the New Testament, no doubt following the example of Jesus himself, celibacy was a genuine and radical alternative (1 Corinthians 7:1–8, 25–40). This would have been particularly striking for women. An unmarried woman of marriageable age would have been regarded in many communities as a social danger. But Paul commends the practice as a worthy option, even though (as a seasoned pastor) he knows it is not for everyone, and he knows that marriage produces its own particular distress (1 Corinthians 7:28).

It is simply no good, then, regarding the Old Testament as the book of fierce legalism and the New Testament as the book of soft options and easygoing inclusivity. On the contrary. The New Testament poses the severe challenge: new creation is being launched, and those who follow Jesus are expected to live as members of that new-creation family, models of what the new creation itself is like. This is only possible (to sum up several much longer trains of thought) because of Jesus's victory on the cross, and in the resurrection, over all the powers of evil, and because of the gift of his Spirit to his followers. Even with all that, the way to new-creation life is hard and complex, as the New Testament writings themselves, and those of subsequent Christian teachers, bear witness. But the demand is not slackened. Christianity was not, at the beginning, a "new ethic"—whether easier or harder, or whether imposed with more or less rigor—which one might adopt as an alternative, say, to that of Aristotle or Pythagoras. It was a whole new way of being human, a top-to-bottom revolution in personality and character which demanded that one grow up in one's thinking and reflecting, one's determining and choosing (I have written about this elsewhere; see *After You Believe*).

So where is monogamy laid down as a principle in the New Testament? Precisely in the passages that speak of new creation. The most striking and obvious passage is the one where Jesus is asked point blank about divorce. The context hints at a political setup: everyone knew about Herod Antipas taking his brother Philip's wife, and everyone knew that Jesus's cousin John the Baptist had been imprisoned and then beheaded for speaking out against precisely this. Would Jesus fall into the same trap?

Not in public, he wouldn't. Later, "in the house," the disciples press him for more detail, and he comes out with it: divorce and remarriage constitutes adultery (Mark 10:10–12). This is parallel to those scenes elsewhere in the gospel where Jesus says something striking but cryptic and then explains the politically sensitive point to the disciples behind closed doors (e.g., Mark 7:17–23). But out in the open Jesus contents himself with laying down the first principle:

Some Pharisees approached him with a question. "Is it permitted," they asked, "for a man to divorce his wife?" They said this to trap him.

"Well," answered Jesus, "what did Moses command you?"

"Moses permitted us," they replied, "to write a notice of separation and so to complete the divorce."

"He gave you that command," said Jesus, "because you are hardhearted. But from the beginning of creation 'male and female he made them; and that's why the man must leave his father and his mother and cleave unto his wife; so that the two become one flesh.'

"There you are, then: they are no longer two, but one flesh. What God has joined, humans must not split up."

(Mark 10:2–9)

This is a crucial passage, actually, for the whole question of a Christian reading of the complete Bible. *Moses gave you that command . . . but from the beginning of creation . . . :* Jesus is saying that the entire Mosaic code was, in principle, a temporary dispensation, designed to advance a larger project which has now arrived, namely the renewal of the whole creation, the restarting of the project sketched in Genesis 1 and 2. In terms of the five-act play I mentioned earlier, this means that Jesus (in Act 4) is claiming that with his arrival the temporary dispensation of the Mosaic Law (part of Act 3) has done its God-given job, and is now to give way to the main cause to which it was always ancillary, namely, the rescuing and restarting of the project begun in Act 1 but aborted or distorted because of Act 2. Act 3 was necessary "because you are hardhearted"; but, unless we are to understand that Jesus is simply being cruel ("I know you're hardhearted and won't be able to keep this tough law, but I'm going to insist on it anyway"), we must understand his meaning to be *that he is offering a cure for hardness of heart.* Only when we get our minds around this can we begin to understand the hermeneutical, let alone the moral, challenge we now face. Jesus is saying that we are to read the scriptures as the story of creation and new creation, and to read the specific codes of the Old Testament as provisional and temporary means to that larger end.

This explains, at a stroke, a good deal of Paul's argument—why, for instance, the Israel-specific rules of circumcision and food laws were irrelevant in the new community where Jews and Gentiles came together as one body. But for the question of monogamy the result is fascinating. Jesus and Paul might have been saying to Abraham, Jacob, David, Solomon, and their fellow polygamists what Paul said to the graybeards at Athens: God has overlooked the times of ignorance, but now he is doing a new thing, remaking creation as it was designed to be (see Acts 17:30).

And at the heart of the original creation we find it: man plus woman, the two becoming one. Again, it is Paul who celebrates this most fully, in the spectacular passage in Ephesians 5 that has caused so much heartache among those who regard it as hierarchical or oppressive. Anything less oppressive than the self-sacrificial model of the husband here would be hard to envisage, though that is not my present point. Paul here draws on the same passage from Genesis as Jesus did:

Wives, be subject to your own husbands, as to the Lord. The man, you see, is the head of the woman, just as the Messiah, too, is head of the church. He is himself the saviour of the body. But, just as the church is subject to the Messiah, in the same way women should be subject in everything to their husbands.

Husbands, love your wives, as the Messiah loved the church, and gave himself for it, so that he could make it holy, cleansing it by washing it with water through the word. He did this in order to present the church to himself in brilliant splendour, without a single spot or blemish or anything of the kind—that it might be holy and without blame. That's how husbands ought to love their own wives, just as they love their own bodies.

Someone who loves his wife loves himself. After all, nobody ever hates his own flesh: he feeds it and takes care of it, just as the Messiah does with the church, because we are parts of his body. "That's why a man leaves his father and mother and is joined to his wife, and the two become one flesh."

The hidden meaning in this saying is very deep; but I am reading it as referring to the Messiah and the church. Any-

way, each one of you must love your wife as you love your-
self; and the wife must see that she respects her husband.
(Ephesians 5:22–33)

All this makes the sense it makes if, and only if, (a) the original
creation was good and (b) the creator God is in the business of
remaking it. Both these points have been under attack in recent
generations, as they were in the early church.

First, the goodness of creation. Some have tried to reintroduce
a dualism not unlike that of the early Gnostics, for whom creation (space, time, and matter—and, particularly, the whole messy
business of sex and reproduction) was basically evil, and salvation
consisted of being rescued from it. That could lead, and did lead,
in one of two directions: either to an asceticism which shunned as
much bodily pleasure as possible, or to a libertinism which declared
that since the body was irrelevant and nonsensical, it did no harm
to indulge its desires—and to the sense that the physical body,
being an irrelevance, provided in itself no guide, no "natural law,"
by which to discern what sexual behavior was appropriate and
what was not. But for the early Christians, with Jesus leading the
way, these options were ruled out. The original creation, with the
male-female human pair as the crown of that creation, and their
bonding as the sign and symbol of the other bondings in the story,
including ultimately heaven and earth itself, was good and would
be reaffirmed. (We might also note that it was their sin which made
them ashamed of their genital organs.)

To the second point: the creator God is in the business of
remaking the original creation, not abandoning it. This principle,
so deeply woven into the New Testament, has often been obscured
by the legacies of different types of dualism, which have had this in
common, that they have seen salvation in terms of humans (per-

haps "souls") being rescued *from* creation rather than of creation itself being rescued and remade. But once again the early Christians were all clear on the point, again following Jesus himself and in particular reflecting on the significance of his resurrection. That was the launching point, the beginning of God's making of all things new.

The goal of that whole project is sketched in Revelation 21 and 22, which constitute the ultimate answer to all forms of Gnosticism. The God of the Bible is not in the business either of abandoning or of destroying his creation. He is in the business of saving it and reestablishing it. And when he does so, the great image which Revelation picks up from numerous earlier biblical sources, particularly the Old Testament's picture of Israel as YHWH's bride, is that of the marriage—not only of heaven and earth, but more specifically, as with Paul in Ephesians 5, of Christ and the church.

This imagery is not accidental. The New Testament writers knew clearly and easily what it has taken contemporary scholars a long time to puzzle out, against the dark undertow of generations of dualistic exegesis: the point of the whole Christian project is not to develop or propound a new ethic or a new way of keeping an old one, nor yet to offer a new spirituality with different patterns of prayer, nor yet, even, to propose a new method of "going to heaven." All of those come into the eventual picture, but none catches its heart. The heart of early Christianity was the belief that in Jesus of Nazareth the creator God had dealt with the rebellion and corruption of the present creation, particularly of the humans who were supposed to be in charge of it, and had opened up the new and living way into a new and living creation *in which the original intention would now be fulfilled.* And that is why, despite the centuries of apparently unrebuked polygamy in the Old Testament, the New Testament assumes on every page that monogamy is now mandatory for the followers of Jesus—and made possible, though as the disciples recognized still difficult (Matthew 19:10), by the victory of Jesus on the cross and the power of his Spirit.

All this opens up a subsequent question, which though important cannot be dealt with here in any detail. If this is so—if monogamy is ultimately part of the new creation—then why should non-Christians be required to undertake it, even if (through divorce and remarriage) they do so serially? This question is cognate with the many similar ones which emerge in the public life of today's post-Christian Western world: Why should the state enforce the specifically Christian (and also Jewish) respect for the life of unborn children, or of the aged and infirm? Why should Christians expect other people to keep "their" way of life?

Each of the many questions that come up in this way has its own unique dynamic, and this is no exception. It remains the case, despite the prevalence of polygamy in some cultures and at least the possibility of it in others, that most cultures in human history, up to the present day, have gravitated toward monogamy and stayed there. There is, it seems, something very powerful about the unique bonding of a man and a woman, however much other pressures can then come in to break it up. It is as though most humans know in their bones that this is, indeed, one of the foundations of wise and healthy human living. In fact, "in their bones" may be literal fact (once we include blood, nerves, and so on as well): this may be a knowledge which literally resides in the body itself, rather than simply an idea which some people have in their heads.

But that is beside the point. The real point, which is also a signpost to many other issues when people ask "Why should Christian morality be good for non-Christians?" is the Christian claim that in Jesus of Nazareth the creator of the world—the whole world, not a Christian subset of the world!—is being rescued and renewed. Of course, non-Christians will say they don't believe this. But Christians do, or at least should—and are therefore committed to believing that the new creation launched in Jesus is good news for *all* people at *every* level, so that even if people do not share explicit Christian faith it will still be a better, wiser, and fairer world if people live with the grain of the universe, which we see in Jesus and in the way of life he modeled and articulated.

I can see a time coming when, in relation to monogamy as many other things, people will no longer be willing to accept this. The rise of polyamory, which I mentioned at the start of this chapter, indicates that some are already starting to think of themselves as naturally nonmonogamous, and we should expect to see a more strident affirmation of this new kind of identity politics, as people claim that their very nature is polygamous, polyandrous, polyamorous, or whatever. The Christian, rooted in the New Testament, would still say that these instincts, though no doubt deep rooted—and, as we all now know, sexual instincts and learned behavior patterns run very deep, so that they do indeed present themselves as being part of the very fiber of one's being—are nevertheless symptomatic of a still-disordered humanity. In terms of Mark 10:5, they reflect a "hardness of heart." Regulations need to be in place so that society can cope with this hard-heartedness. But the vision persists, of the original intention for creation and the possibility of that vision being recaptured. Future debates will need to focus on the awkward gap between theory and practice, both within Christian communities—couples and individual hearts—and within wider non-Christian communities—couples and individuals as well. But the underlying point should be clear. Monogamy, from the Christian point of view, is the one and only appropriate alternative to celibacy.

What has this taught us, or illustrated, about "scripture and the authority of God"? First, it has emphatically underlined the point that one simply cannot see the Bible "in the flat," with something being validated or somehow even ennobled just because it is in the Bible. The attempt—whether on flaky websites or in apparently more serious projects—to argue that what we find in the Bible is somehow thereby validated must be challenged, not because the Bible is not the book God intends us to have but because God intends that we use our prayerful and Spirit-informed minds as we read this book. Rather, second, we must once more see the Bible as a *story* with different movements, a play in different acts, and we must understand the whole story in terms of the climax which is reached in Act 4 and the resultant resolution, and the restoration of the original project, in Act 5. Thus, though in the Bible we do indeed find a good deal of polygamy, including among people with whom God was doing serious business, we must affirm on the basis of Jesus's own teaching and, still more, his creation-rescuing and creation-renewing accomplishment, that scripture read wisely as the narrative it really is points clearly and decisively to monogamy as the proper calling of those who are not called to celibacy.

I end where I began. This may seem a surprising discussion, in that few Western people today stop to question monogamy. Few actually advocate polygamy (though obviously some do), but few would know how to argue from the authority of scripture against a well-researched polygamist. But when we approach the question of scripture's authority, as I have tried to do throughout this book, in the light of the whole story and intention of the creator God, dealing with his world step-by-step and eventually dealing decisively with it in and through Jesus Christ, then we discover that the authority of God, as mediated through and in the whole scripture, points to the renewal of creation through Jesus Christ as the key theme of the whole story. And within that renewal, the renewal of monogamy, and the invitation to celebrate lifelong marriage not only in itself but also as one of the clearest signposts to the creator's intention for the whole world, stands out clear and sharp. Monogamy is a pointer to one of today's urgently needed cosmic truths: the creator's purpose is not to split heaven and earth apart, but rather to bring them together in a costly but wonderfully enriching unity (Ephesians 1:10). That purpose, already realized in Jesus Christ, is signaled, embodied, and advanced in monogamous marriage.

APPENDIX

Recent Resources on Scripture

Getting Started on Bible Study

Those who want to get into the study of scripture for themselves—and studying scripture is, in the end, far more profitable than theorizing about it—will find a wealth of material to help them. What follows is only a small selection, which could be supplemented almost indefinitely by a visit to a good Christian bookshop or any of several bookselling websites.

New *translations* of the Bible continue to appear. For study purposes, assuming the reader does not have access to the original languages, the New Revised Standard Version is increasingly accepted in both church and academy. It is not without its faults, and not all of its attempts to avoid gender-specific language are as felicitous as they might be. The English Standard Version follows the tradition of the Revised Standard Version closely, but has continued to use gender-specific language. The New International Version, even in its updated format, is popular, but still has several weaknesses, particularly in its handling of Paul. The New American Standard Version has become widely used, and well spoken of, in North America.

There are many series of *commentaries* on, and guides to, individual books. Here I need only to mention a few at the more popular end of the market; those who want scholarly discussion of particular books and passages will not need me to tell them where to find it. My own "Everyone" series on the New Testament (*Matthew for Everyone*, etc., published by SPCK and WJKP, and including a fresh translation) is nearing completion. The Tyndale series, published by Inter-Varsity Press in the United Kingdom and Eerdmans in the United States, has some fine volumes, and is being steadily updated to meet the needs of a new generation of biblical beginners. The Interpretation series of commentaries, published by John Knox Press, has a fine track record for clear, wise, and helpful discussion of the text. The *Black's New Testament Commentaries,* published now by Continuum, offer a slightly more academic treatment and are likewise being updated. The *New Interpreter's Bible,* published by Abingdon, is a first-rate twelve-volume set, covering the whole Bible and the Apocrypha. Two of the best of the one-volume Bible commentaries are the *HarperCollins Bible Commentary,* edited by James L. Mays, and the *Oxford Bible Commentary,* edited by John Barton and John Muddiman.

Beginners and seasoned readers alike ought to possess a Bible dictionary. The best of these include the five-volume *New Interpreters Dictionary of the Bible,* edited by K. D. Sakenfeld (Abingdon, 2006–09). There are two recent one-volume dictionaries: the *HarperCollins Bible Dictionary* (revised and updated edition), edited by Mark Allan Powell, and the *Eerdmans Dictionary of the Bible,* edited by D. N. Freedman. The volumes published by Inter-Varsity Press (USA) (*Dictionary of the Old Testament,* in three volumes; *Dictionary of Jesus and the Gospels; Dictionary of Paul and His Letters; Dictionary of the Later New Testament and Its Developments;* and *Dictionary of New Testament Background*) are packed full of useful material. So is the *Dictionary for Theological Interpretation of the Bible,* edited by Kevin J. Vanhoozer and published by Baker Academic. For matters of wider interest that emerge when people study the Bible, I have constantly referred to *The Oxford Dictionary of the Christian Church,* edited by F. L. Cross and E. A. Livingstone (third edition), and *The Oxford Companion to Christian Thought,* edited by Adrian Hastings.

Many printed Bibles contain maps, but these are often small and somewhat perfunctory. Anyone wanting to come to grips with where the biblical events took place should acquire one of the relevant atlases. There are many available, among which I merely mention the *Oxford Bible Atlas,* edited by H. G. May (third edition), the *HarperCollins Concise Atlas of the Bible,* edited by J. Pritchard, or indeed the remarkable *Aerial Atlas of the Holy Land,* edited by John Bowker (London: Octopus Publishing, 2008).

Following Up on Themes in the Present Book

Those who want to follow up on the subject of the present book at a more academic level, or who want to see the kind of work with which I am in implicit dialogue throughout it, may find the following of interest:

I presuppose the massive survey of hermeneutics offered by A. C. Thiselton in his *New Horizons in Hermeneutics* (HarperCollins, 1992) and the distinctive contribution of Nicholas Wolterstorff in his *Divine Discourse* (CUP, 1995). Francis Watson's two books *Text and Truth* (Eerdmans, 1997) and *Text, Church and World* (T. & T. Clark, 1994) offer several fresh lines of inquiry. Frances Young's book *The Art of Performance* (DLT, 1990) was a breath of fresh air, encouraging me to pursue certain lines further.

Other important, more recent works include Kevin J. Vanhoozer, *Is There a Meaning in This Text?* (Zondervan, 1998) and *First Theology: God, Scripture and Hermeneutics* (IVP, 2002); Gerard Loughlin, *Telling God's Story: Bible, Church and Narrative Theology* (CUP, 1998); Stephen Fowl, *Engaging Scripture: A Model for Theological Interpretation* (Blackwell, 1998); William J. Abraham, *Canon and Criterion in Christian Theology: From the Fathers to Feminism* (OUP, 1998); John Webster, *Holy Scripture: A Dogmatic Sketch* (CUP, 2003); and several books by Richard J. Bauckham, including *The Bible in Politics* (WJKP, 1990), *God and the Crisis of Freedom: Biblical and Contemporary Perspectives* (WJKP, 2002), and *Bible and Mission: Christian Witness in a Postmodern World* (Paternoster/Baker, 2003).

Three other recent books which open up fresh and creative windows on the whole topic are Telford Work, *Living and Active: Scripture in the Economy of Salvation* (Eerdmans, 2002); Ellen F. Davis and Richard B. Hays (eds.), *The Art of Reading Scripture* (Eerdmans, 2003); and David Lyle Jeffries, *Houses of the Interpreter: Reading Scripture, Reading Culture* (Baylor University Press, 2003). Several important essays on similar subjects are collected in Joel B. Green and Max Turner (eds.), *Between Two Horizons: Spanning New Testament Studies and Systematic Theology* (Eerdmans, 2000). Of particular note, showing lively and high-level engagement with all the relevant issues, is the series on scripture and hermeneutics, edited by Craig Bartholomew and others (Paternoster/Zondervan), with five substantial volumes already published (*Renewing Biblical Interpretation*, 2000; *After Pentecost*, 2001; *A Royal Priesthood?* 2002; *Behind the Text*, 2003; *Out of Egypt*, 2004) and more promised.

SCRIPTURE INDEX

SUBJECT INDEX

Abraham: covenant between God and, 33–34, 54, 55; polygamy practiced by, 179, 184, 188

Abrahams, Harold, 146

adultery, 181, 182, 187

African Christians, 176

After You Believe (Wright), 164, 171, 186

allegorical exegesis: medieval allegorical sense of scripture, 69–71; Old Testament and New Testament, 66–68

anagogical sense of scripture, 69

Anglican Communion, 131

Apostles' Creed, 119

Aquinas. *See* Thomas Aquinas

Augustine, 2, 165

authority: of accredited church leaders, 139–42; distinguishing devotion from, 30; of God's Kingdom, 26–28; God as source of all, 21–23; questions regarding Bible, 16; scripture used to direct God's, 23, 27–28, 38, 131–33, 137–38; scripture as vehicle for church, 51–52, 65–66; of tradition and scripture, 76

authority of scripture: authoritative Bible stories expressions of, 23–25; examining the meaning of, 21–23; experience role in, 100–105; as function of authority of Jesus, 172; God's authority and mission directed through, 23, 27–28, 38, 131–33, 137–38; improvisation notion of, 127, 128; Jesus's insistence on the, 43–45; as language of protest, 25–26; meaning and implications of, 115–18; as means to operate story of Bible, 171–72; mod-

ern biblical studies context of, 90–93; monogamy understood through, 175–95; reason and rationality role in, 78–81, 84–87, 120–21; role of tradition in, 71–72, 118–20, 130–33; sabbath understood through, 143–73; second-Temple Judaism and, 38–39; story of creation/renewed creation, and covenant focus of, 141–42, 161–66, 173, 190–91, 194–95; strategies for honoring the, 128–42; as sub-branch of other theological topics, 27–28; tradition role in, 71–72, 118–20, 130–33. *See also* reading scripture; scripture narrative

Barth, Karl, 13, 18

Bathsheba, 181

Bible: allegorical exegesis of the, 66–68; authoritative stories of the, 23–25; implications of church role of, 31–32; key questions about the, 16; political context of, 9; questions regarding the authority of the, 16; understood as a story, 171–72. *See also* New Testament; Old Testament; scripture

biblicalpolygamy.com, 183–84

biblical scholarship: avoiding the shallow aspects of, 18–19; "battles for the Bible" in, 1, 16–17; current state of modern, 90–93; Enlightenment's rationalism as part of, 78–81, 84–90, 101–2, 110; non-literalist/literalist polarization of, 93–94; postmodernity's deconstruction contribution to,

DATE DUE